Walter Matthau

Walter Matthau

Allan Hunter

St. Martin's Press
New York

Library of Congress Cataloging in Publication Data

Hunter, Allan, 1961-
  Walter Matthau.

  1. Matthau, Walter. 2. Actors—United States—
Biography. I. Title.
PN2287.M543H8 1985   792'.028'0924 [B]   84-22856
ISBN 0-312-85519-2

First published in Great Britain by W.H. Allen & Co. Limited.

First U.S. Edition

10 9 8 7 6 5 4 3 2 1

Acknowledgements

When Walter Matthau was approached about co-operating in a book on his life and career he replied; 'I am not yet ready for biographies and such. Give me another 25 years and you will have my assistance and my approval.' This book then is the result of research from Matthau's magazine and newspaper interviews, the comments of his colleagues and viewings of his films.

I would like to thank the following among Matthau's colleagues for taking the time to respond to queries: Richard Benjamin, Carol Burnett, Glenda Jackson, Jack Lemmon and Maureen Stapleton even if, in some cases, they felt unable to co-operate in anything that Matthau had not sanctioned himself. Thanks too, to the producer-director Stanley Jaffe for taking a break from the Edinburgh Film Festival to discuss his work with Matthau.

I am indebted to the various departments of the British Film Institute and the National Film Archive for their enthusiasm, courtesy and knowledge, the same qualities to be found among the people at the Kobal Collection. The following individuals were invaluable during research; Barbara de Lord of Columbia-EMI-Warner for providing useful information, flatmates

Roddy, Penny, Phil and John for being understanding and, as usual, my parents for being supportive and encouraging.

A final and deeply felt thanks goes to the book's editor Amanda Girling for having faith.

Allan Hunter

Chapter One

'Anything I tell you in the next hour is only going to be lies,' was Walter Matthau's greeting to one interviewer and, whilst no similar claims are made for this book, there are more than the usual number of red herrings encountered in detailing Matthau's story. He has a style of exaggerating an incident, embellishing an anecdote in the retelling and generally putting someone off the scent should they tread too close. His birthdate, for instance, is widely quoted as being 1920 yet in recent years, he has maintained that the year is 1923, and once admiringly referred to a copy of *Who's Who in the Theatre* which stated 1925.

The America of the 1920s was a country of sharp contrasts – a heterogeneous society of haves and have nots, of great affluence and extreme poverty. The period was one of a certain static social stability in which the rich stayed rich and the poor stayed poor. In 1920 the Republican Party gained a landslide victory electing Ohio Senator Warren G. Harding to the country's highest office and ending the eight-year presidency of Woodrow Wilson. In January of that year the 18th (Prohibition) Amendment to the Constitution came into effect and the country went 'dry'. Alcohol became a forbidden fruit tempting the average American into illegal speakeasies and bootleg gin, and heralding the rise of gangsterism. The technical revolution was upon the land and the decade saw a vast rise in the use of cars, telephones and electricity. In November, 1920 the first broadcasting station opened in Pittsburgh and one car in two throughout the world was one of Henry Ford's Model Ts. The rich amused themselves as flappers danced to the Charleston and the Black Bottom whilst the country as a whole displayed an insatiable appetite for larger-than-life heroes like aviator Charles Lindbergh, the New York Yankees Babe Ruth and evangelist Aimee Semple McPherson. Silent movies entered a golden era with ordinary people standing in line for the swashbuckling feats of Douglas Fairbanks Snr in *The Mark of Zorro* and the latest antics of Charlie Chaplin in *The Kid*. America, it seemed, was still the land of opportunity and the twenties was an exciting time in which to grow up.

Walter Matuschanskayasky, one of the have nots, was born on 1 October 1920 in New York City. According to Matthau's own version of his early years his father, Milton, was a Russian orthodox priest who had fled to New York with his mother Rose, but deserted the family when Matthau was only three. His parents had formed part of the great mass of immigrants which flooded into the country from southern and eastern Europe. Attracted by visions of America as the promised land, free from religious persecution and teeming with employment opportunities, the Europeans had arrived in their millions. Years later Matthau commented: 'When my mother came to the States from Lithuania, they told her the streets were paved with gold. She's still looking for it.'

The population of New York State in 1920 was over ten million and very few found their personal pot of gold. The average immigrant family from Russia or Poland arrived in America with little English, no money and no accommodation. They could rarely afford to move further than their point of disembarkation, New York, and many thousands crowded into the squalor of the city's tenements. From the youngest to the oldest it was necessary to find work; usually manual and invariably low paid.

Walter lived a penurious existence with his mother and elder brother Henry in the tough, lower East side of New York City. His father had earned a living as an odd job man and later as a server of summonses. 'Used to disguise himself as a telegram deliverer and hand out summonses instead,' Matthau would recall. 'He died at forty-six. He ran away from my mother, which was actually the only thing he could do. She was a beautiful, big-bosomed, vital lady who thought sex was dirty. Poor guy must have gone crazy.'

His mother worked in a sweatshop in the city's garment district, enduring the daily grind at her sewing machine to provide the family's income. The early years were marked by a series of hasty flittings to keep one step ahead of the rent collector. The young Walter and brother Henry became day boarders at the Daughter of Israel Nursery which charged a dollar a week. It was there, at the age of four, that he made his first stage appearance in one of the nursery's religious plays.

His childhood provides glimpses of the early stages in what would become two of the great passions of his life; performing and gambling. At the time, and for quite a while to come, it was gambling that exerted the stronger hold. Extreme poverty, it seems, results in one of two attitudes towards money; either you become neurotic and thrifty or you can't dispose of it quickly enough. Given Matthau's success as a gambler he obviously belongs to the latter category. A childhood spent on the

9

East side wouldn't have been complete without hanging around with other kids, making a little bet and trying to strike it rich. He once told a British interviewer how the gambling fever had first struck. 'I was an urchin, selling candy at 6d a time. By the end of the day I'd be rich, with maybe £1 to spend on myself. I'd change out of my clothes into a good suit, give a dollar to my mother, spend a few cents on a hamburger and a glass of milk, and then I'd be up on the roof tops for seven-up or twenty-one with the neighbourhood guys. That was the start of it all – and I'd lose even then!'

Interestingly enough, his brother Henry chose to look after every cent and Matthau describes him as a 'normal, straight, lower East side boy with no illusions, but I always had these dreams.'

At nursery school he had read poems at assembly but his first real brush with the stage and its inhabitants came when he began working the candy and soft drinks concessions in the Yiddish-language theatres in New York's Second Avenue. He worked selling candy and cherry pop for three or four years and would sit enthralled by the thrill of watching actors close-up. Eventually, having been around the place for so long he was asked to participate in the occasional crowd scene and began being given the odd line of dialogue to say. He gained a small part in the play *The Dishwasher* and was paid fifty cents per performance, seven performances a week.

'I was always an enterprising little kid, always trying to learn things to bluff my way through new experiences,' he said. 'I once worked as a youngster in a theatre where they spoke Yiddish. I got a job there selling ice-cream and cold drinks, and I picked up little snippets of the language. Then I went to another theatre where they spoke Italian. I sold bags of sugar-coated peanuts and picked up that lingo. Then I went back to the Yiddish theatre and got a job as an actor speaking the lines in Yiddish based on what I'd picked up while I sold ice-cream. I played my first role there at the wee age of eleven – I was an old woman in a crowd scene!'

Enterprising as ever, he would still exercise his refreshment concession earning another $2.50 in a good week. It provided a glamorous escape from everyday cares and Matthau loved every moment: 'I used to feel marvellous just being in the theatre. In high school I began reading a lot of Shakespeare, reading the poems and the plays out loud to myself. 'When he was fourteen he appeared in a Settlement House production of *Hamlet* as Polonius, the Lord Chamberlain.

The main influence in his early life was his mother Rose, and his stories about her are legion. He claims: 'My mother was the worst cook in the country, maybe even in the entire world. She thought all blood must be thoroughly cooked out of meat. As a result, three times a week I had shoe leather for dinner.' More seriously, he believes, 'In this atmosphere of misery and sadness I was the only one in the world able to make my mother laugh. She was my first public. Her smile was the greatest reward for me. They were hard years as I look back. I suppose when you are in it you have the advantage of ignorance and youth and you didn't mind much. When you lose those qualities you still have to maintain a certain level. Otherwise it is too unbearable.'

Ironically, a childhood of extreme poverty in a New York–Jewish milieu was probably what helped him foster his sense of timing and humour. Instead of meeting hardship with despair, you crack a joke and provide a veneer of levity to mask the true despair. His youth was a breeding ground for that particular form of gallows humour where if you don't laugh you would

11

surely be in tears. Not so coincidentally Neil Simon, Matthau's junior by several years, grew up in similar circumstances – another one of the have nots. It is not surprising that the two collaborated to such memorable effect years later.

One journalist claims that, at the age of nine, Matthau was determined to pursue a career as either an actor or a writer. Such claims can probably be dismissed as Hollywood exaggeration. However, exaggeration not that far removed from reality. Matthau remembers no such burning desire, professing instead to have 'congealed' into the profession of actor. As a youth he seems fairly content to have drifted along. An athletic six foot, three inches, he acted in school plays at Seward Park High and lettered in varsity basketball, track, soccer and swimming. His tough upbringing had not only formed his character but also helped to mould the generously proportioned Matthau proboscis. 'From the time I was nine my peculiar nose was good for a fist fight every day or so. And while it didn't start off being exactly Grecian, it was hit so often that it got even more oversized,' he says.

As a schoolboy Matthau enjoyed the shared interests of his peers; sports and gambling. However, he was extremely shy and did enjoy his forays into acting as a way of expressing himself through an assumed persona. 'I appeared relaxed but I was shy. It's always the introverts who look for a means of expression. My brother was the one everybody thought would be an actor. I always liked to perform. As I got older I began imitating movie stars a lot. It made other kids laugh. I was constantly dreaming. God knows of what. Not fantasies of having a great career in the theatre. Just . . . fantasies. I always tried to speak well, instinctively. Kids would say to Henry, "Whatsa mattuh with yuh brudder?

He talks funny. Izzy from outa town?"'

He graduated from High School in 1939 and over the next three years held a variety of fairly menial jobs. Initially he joined the Civilian Conservation Corps, a government sponsored programme for unemployed youth. The list of jobs he subsequently secured is lengthy: he scrubbed floors in a Manhattan factory, worked as a lumberjack in Montana, a boxing instructor, baseball coach and cement hauler. The most improbable occupation with which he has been credited is an oven-cleaner with a doll manufacturing company.

Walter was obviously leading a directionless life, with no ambitions for a set career. If he was to become an actor or writer he needed to gain some experience or at least a basic grounding in either profession, and he could probably afford neither the time nor the investment to pursue such a notion. However, any such dilemma was firmly put to one side when America entered the Second World War. In April 1942 Matthau, aged twenty-one, enlisted in the Air Force.

His war was both exciting and dangerous, broadening his horizons and leaving him more firmly resolved to pursue the ambition to write or perform. Pressed to discuss his war years he would comment: 'I came to Britain in 1943 and was stationed at Bovington and then in Norfolk. My job was to teach instrumental take-off to American pilots. I went to France in '44, then Belgium and Holland. I flew four missions but the rest was general training stuff. Which was good because all those planes were getting shot out of the sky. We always had new personnel coming in.'

What he generally failed to mention were the six battle stars he earned – they were usually dismissed with a comment like: 'During World Two I was ping pong champion of the Armed Forces.' As a radio operator and cryptographer he served with distinction and it is characteristic that he should belittle his war record.

Among the other personnel at 505 wing of the 453rd Bomber Squadron was James Stewart, who had been one of the first major Hollywood stars to enlist. 'He was a colonel and I was a staff sergeant. We didn't have a lot to do with each other. He would turn up with a few generals to see how things were going. I think I once got into a volleyball game with him.' Matthau was prone to imitations of the older, Oscar-winning actor's slow drawl and is convinced that Stewart influenced his final decision to become an actor. In later years Stewart, in all honesty, had no recollections of the sergeant who served under him.

The acting bug found other outlets during the wartime years, apart from his Stewart imitations. 'We were stationed in Norfolk and one evening I went into Norwich to see *Arsenic and Old Lace*. In those days there was even entertainment during the intermission and we had a magician on stage,' he has explained. 'He asked for a volunteer, as magicians so often do, and I put my hand up and ambled down the aisle. The audience started shouting, "Get along . . . hurry up . . .", but I just kept going, nice and steady, and by the time I had reached the magician I had got a pretty good laugh. It's an old comic trick: When you're in the public view behave as though you are not.'

The gambling urge had also persisted and, indirectly, led to a decision regarding his future career. Having coached in basketball and boxing, his service record listed his civilian occupation as 'Recreation aide'. It seemed likely that he would return to similar pursuits on his discharge. 'At the end of the war there was a job lined up for me as a Boy Scout Co-ordinator at $1800 a year with a car and a house. But a girl in the British Red Cross, who was my first big affair, pointed out that it was at Tonopah, Nevada, and that every time I came in from the desert I'd lose all my money at the gaming tables. She told me to go to New York and either do a course in acting or journalism.' That was exactly what he did.

why was I not seeing them, noticed our first meteor in _____ dormant _____ blazkly, and their _____ _____. _____ is _____. the _____ _____ my _____ of _____ _____ _____ could never tell to the _____ _____ _____ _____ _____ _____ _____ _____ _____ _____ _____ _____ _____ _____ _____

Chapter Two

In 1944 the American Congress passed the Serviceman's Re-adjustment Act, which became known as the GI Bill of Rights, and allocated Government provisions for aid to veterans' hospitals and vocational rehabilitation as well as allowing for the purchase by veterans of houses, farms and businesses. The most relevant segment of the act for Matthau was the provision of funds for four years of college education, an allowance of $500 a year for tuition and books with monthly expenses of $50 (later $65). It was a grateful Government's reward for the men and boys who had journeyed 'over there' to fight the Fascist menace and, for the returning Matthau, it was an unexpected passport to enter the world of journalism or acting, avenues that might otherwise have remained blocked for purely financial reasons. The passing of the GI Bill of Rights is probably as instrumental as anything else in Matthau's becoming an actor.

At first he leaned towards journalism and studied briefly at Columbia with a career as a newspaperman in mind. The reasons for his swift reversal to a commitment towards acting can only be speculated upon, but as an introvert, Matthau must have realised the wonderful opportunities inherent in the make-believe world of acting which enabled you to hide behind a character and disguise your timidity by assuming any number of

17

varied roles. It's a view he tends to confirm in some later statements – in 1980 he told one interviewer, 'If you think I've got *savoir faire*, I guess I'm a better actor than I think I am. Actually I never say anything I don't mean. And if I tell you I'm shy you'd better believe it. Why do you think I decided to become an actor in the first place? For the applause? Forget it. I became an actor, or should I say "congealed" into one, as a sort of defence mechanism. When you're on stage or on a movie set with all those bright lights shining in your eyes you don't see a damn thing except the other actors. For a shy person it's a marvellous form of escape.'

He enrolled at the Dramatic Workshop of the New School for Social Research in New York and, 'began learning what it was all about. We had great teachers there. I just enjoyed being at drama school after four years in the Air Corps. Practically anything at all was a gift after that!' Still an avid gambler he was also attracted to the Workshop because of its proximity to Madison Square Garden, a haven of sports fixtures and prize fights. 'I didn't want to miss too many events', he said.

The Workshop was run by the German-born Erwin Piscator who had come to America in the late thirties, gaining his entry under the quota system. That same system did not permit him to settle in his adopted land as a theatre director but only as a teacher. The New School in New York was an adult education college that supported Piscator by establishing the Dramatic Workshop especially for him. Piscator was to run the Workshop from its opening in 1940 until 1951. His view of theatre was that is should encompass not only entertainment but also the pressing social and political issues of the day. The stated aim of the workshop was to provide, 'a school that is a theatre and a theatre that is a school', and 'to stimulate the development of the repertory theatre as a non-commercial institution of artistic expression with the same position in our society that the symphony or the art museum enjoys.'

Immediately after the war the Workshop reached a peak of activity with almost 1000 students in attendance. In the early years there had been around twenty students attending evening classes where the main focus was on the development of playwriting skills. Among the first-year students then was Tennessee Williams. The Workshop gradually expanded. In 1944, Marlon Brando studied there under Stella Adler, a teacher in the Stanislavsky method of acting. During Matthau's period at the Workshop there were a variety of teaching styles on offer, ranging from Piscator, who liked to involve his pupils in all aspects of stage presentation, to the 'Method' school of thought that Lee Strasberg advocated in his acting and directing classes. Piscator called for objectivity in acting, where the performer is aware of the audience and plays to them, whereas the Stanislavsky method is one of seeking a realism and naturalism which comes from within, from the experiences of the actor, experiences which he can use to explore the motivations and actions of his character.

Matthau absorbed the Workshop's teachings and participated in the students' public performances which attempted to involve the audience in the whole theatrical experience by having open rehearsals, lectures on the plays and post-performance discussions. Among Matthau's fellow students were Rod Steiger, Eli Wallach, Gene Saks, Harry Belafonte and Tony Curtis, then studying under his real name of Bernard Schwartz. Between 1947 and 1948, Matthau performed opposite Elaine Stritch in Lillian Hellman's *The Little Foxes*.

In many ways the Dramatic Workshop has been given its place in American theatre history as a predecessor of the famed Actors Studio, and Matthau certainly seems to have appreciated the socialist view of a people's theatre for the whole community, as well as appreciating the quality of the teachers. At times, however, he has expressed alarm at Piscator's predilection for the technological side of the theatre: 'I studied with the great Erwin Piscator. I have heard Piscator say he wished he could put on plays with just turntables, screens, projection machines, light effects – without one actor, because, my God, actors got in his way!'

In the post-war years Matthau interspersed his studies by learning his craft at a variety of professional assignments including summer stock at the County Playhouse in Erie, Pennsylvania, where he played the role of Charlie in *Three Men on a Horse* and featured in *Ten Nights in a Bar Room*. In succeeding summers he was engaged by the Orange County Playhouse in New York and played summer stock again at Southold on Long Island. To supplement his income he waited on tables and worked at some dead-end jobs to keep the wolf from the door, and at one stage he was a brush salesman and a shipping clerk. He also managed to pick up some roles on network television. In the immediate post-war years television was still very much an infant medium regarded with lofty disdain by most established stars. For Matthau, and many other performers of his generation, television became a constant source of employment and acting opportunities.

Then, in 1948, he gained his first Broadway role in *Anne of a Thousand Days*, one of the year's major plays. Written by Maxwell Anderson, who had a distinguished record of historical dramas including one on Mary of Scotland and one on Elizabeth, the Queen, the production of *Anne of a Thousand Days* was entrusted to agent turned producer Leland Hayward. A complicated saga about Henry VIII's marriage to Anne Boleyn, the play involved flashbacks from the present to the past and back again which involved the technical challenges of an intricate number of revolving stages and moving chairs. Rex Harrison was cast as Henry, Joyce Redman as his queen and Bretaigne Windust would direct.

Matthau was the understudy for seven characters in *Anne of a Thousand Days*. On separate occasions he played the eighty-three-year-old English Bishop Fisher and a candelabrum carrier. There was one part in which he was determined to prove his devotion to his profession, a courier at Henry's court.

Undergoing some fine tuning, the Broadway-bound *Anne of a Thousand Days* played for two weeks in Philadelphia. Matthau would later recall: 'In my very first play I had a fine part as the courier to the Duke of Northumberland which actually included a line of dialogue. I had to come on and say, "I've ridden for thirty-eight hours and I'm dead for sleep," and then I had to collapse right there on the stage.

'I gave that part a lot of dedication. I used to do knee-bends in the wings to get short of breath and make my legs kind of rubbery. On the opening night in Philadelphia I was so keyed up to do a good job I did about a hundred knee-bends and rushed around the theatre to tire myself out. What an idiot! When I made my entrance I fell flat on my face. I had to scream my line from down there and it didn't sound so good.'

True or not, Matthau falling flat on his face wasn't the show's only problem that opening night in Philadelphia. The revolving sets and moving chairs had proved problematic and largely unworkable. The New York opening was postponed for two weeks and the company moved to Baltimore where a specially designed Tudor set and lighting effects provided the mood and time changes to substitute for the more elaborate set in Philadelphia. The Broadway opening, in show parlance, was a smash and a critical success. Rex Harrison went on to win the Antoinette Perry (Tony) Award as Best Actor and the show ran for six months until its summer lay-off the following year. It ran a further four months on its return in September 1949. Way down among the supporting cast it also cemented the love of all things theatrical for one Walter Matthau.

Matthau strived fairly anonymously in the theatre over the next few years, working his way up the ladder in plays like *The Liar* and *Season in the Sun*, to his first leading role in *Twilight Walk*. The same year, 1951, he also starred in *Fancy Meeting You Again* and *One Bright Day*. Much of his work was critically highly regarded; he won the New York Drama Critics award for *Twilight Walk*, and the play *Ladies of the Corridor* was selected by one critic as the best play of 1953. However, they were all flops in the public's eye and it has been estimated that none lasted more than three weeks.

To relax, Matthau continued his sporting interests, playing in the Broadway Show *League*, which was a summertime series of softball games in New York. The teams consisted of willing performers from the shows on Broadway, and the series was not without its hazards, including a memorable run-in between Matthau and Henry Fonda. Fonda was then appearing in the lengthy run of *Mister Roberts* and remembered: 'You'd think with all those brawny young sailors the Roberts team would win every game. But no! We'd get whipped regularly by the chorus boys from *South Pacific* or *Gentlemen Prefer Blondes* or *Peter Pan*.

'In one game, though, when I was at bat, I punched a clean line drive smack into Walter Matthau's balls. He claims I was trying to put him out of commission, right there in front of everybody in Central Park.'

Matthau paid the bills by working intensively in television. The era of the early fifties was later immortalised in the film *My Favourite Year* as a time when 'Television was live and comedy was king'. Comedy may have been king but the dramatic anthology ran a pretty close second. Live drama from New York flourished as never before and brought a whole new generation of performers to the public's attention. The older, more established movie stars largely chose to remain aloof from the rigours of the new medium, whilst the younger performers who were under any form of studio contract were prevented from making appearances. The door was left wide open for a generation of hungry young Broadway and New York actors to stretch their wings and gain experience and exposure before the cameras. Thus Jack Lemmon, Rod Steiger, Paul Newman, Charlton Heston and a host of others could be seen in the various hour and half hour dramatic anthologies that were broadcast live from New York. Shows that Matthau appeared on included the 'Campbell Soundstage' and the 'Goodyear TV Playhouse' which incorporated original plays for the medium by new talents like Paddy Chayevsky, who contributed 'Marty' and 'The Catered Affair'.

The kind of high-adrenalin live television where anything could happen proved an invaluable training ground and source of income. An actor learnt the discipline of not fluffing lines, because there were no retakes, of hitting the right marks and giving cues – all the technical skills of acting for the camera which can take years to acquire from making just a couple of films per annum but which come double-quick to a performer making, in essence, the equivalent of a sixty-minute feature once a month. The whole process sharpened the acting instinct. The medium also allowed a performer such a variety of roles that in 1953 Matthau would appear in an August episode of the Philco Playhouse which was a production of *Othello* and a couple of months later would pop up in the Studio One presentation, 'Dry Run', with Katherine McLeod in 'a tale of derring-do aboard a World War Two submarine'. In later years Matthau would be the guest-star in many of the top-rated television shows including 'Dr Kildare', 'Route 66', 'The Naked City' and 'Alfred Hitchcock Presents'.

In the early fifties Matthau needed both the experience and the money; the need for the latter commodity was particularly acute since he was still a chronic sufferer from the gambling disease. Of this period he has said, 'I honestly believed that the only reason one made money was to give it away to the bookmakers.' His gambling was compulsive and he lost far more often than he won, regarding himself as a born loser. He said in one British interview, 'I remember the first time I went to a greyhound track. I pushed out seventy-five pounds, and my dog stopped and raised its leg in the middle of the race. If I hadn't known I was a loser before, I knew it then. The curious thing is that I enjoyed losing. When I don't gamble I get mean and irritable, and when I win I somehow feel I've cheated.' Over the years he estimates losing something in the region of one and a half million pounds and once gambled a year's salary on the outcome of an exhibition baseball game. A young, promising actor, his gambling fever was another expression of his inbuilt insecurity and partly, he believes, an outcome of the grim poverty of his youth when money took on such a massive significance that the family always lived dangerously. Now that he had some form of income he continued to live on the brink, only now at a more inflated level.

In some circles he was better known as a reckless gambler than for any acting accomplishments. Whilst this lack of recognition is disheartening for any performer it did have one, and only one, advantage. His relative obscurity meant that his socialist views escaped the attention of one Senator Joseph McCarthy and thus the wrath of the House of Un-American Activities and all the repercussions of a loathsome period in American history, of blacklistings and the destruction of careers on the criteria of political sympathies. Matthau can only have been disgusted by the seeming mood of hysteria but masks a genuine concern with a typically light-hearted comment: 'I signed the Stockholm Peace Convention but I have very bad handwriting.'

In the entertainment world of the early fifties the new stars were young, pretty and glamorous – and those were just the male ones. The movie idols required the handsomeness of a Tony Curtis or a Rock Hudson to replace the established box-office stars, brawny men of action like John Wayne, Gable and 'Coop'. Matthau felt himself out of sorts with cinema audience requirements, his lived-in features (once described as 'like one of those amiable inventions used to people Disney cartoons') and shy nature left him with much food for thought in making comparisons with his successful peers.

Regarding himself as a born loser in gambling he was equally self-critical with his assessment of any personal qualities. 'In those days I did a great deal of brooding – I wasn't handsome. I didn't have any good clothes. I used to wonder why people would like me.' Such self-doubting largely fell away when he was on stage, gaining confidence behind a character and responding to the appreciation of his work by colleagues and critics. 'It became apparent that when I got up on a stage, people wanted to look at me. What did I have to offer? I was a big rugged-looking guy with a big, strong voice. There was that. Also I had a way of showing enormous ease and enormous power on stage, both of which were valuable in the theatre.'

Matthau was obviously a talented performer, who, as yet, lacked the public recognition that would establish him as a star. He found little in his private life to compensate for this as he continued a harsh self-appraisal and was unable to curb his self-destructive gambling urge.

It is said that any actor can point to an event, person or period that forms a crossroads or turning point in their lives. In Matthau's story it is possible to pinpoint two such moments, crucial to his life, and the first came in 1955.

Chapter Three

1955 is a special year in Matthau's life for a number of reasons. Firstly, there was a play called *Will Success Spoil Rock Hunter?* by George Axelrod. Born in New York, two years after Matthau and with Russian blood from his grandfather, Axelrod and Matthau shared a common background and upbringing. Axelrod entered the showbusiness world as an assistant stage manager and, after working in radio and television as a gag writer and concocting material for the Dean Martin-Jerry Lewis comedy duo, he wrote his first play *The Seven Year Itch*, one of the big hits of 1952. *Will Success Spoil Rock Hunter?* was the follow-up: an astringent satire dealing with a massive television advertising company and how one employee, a shy ideas man, persuades a glamorous Hollywood sex symbol to endorse a lipstick before escaping the rat race for life down on the farm.

The play was another hit for Axelrod, and Matthau's featured role was rewarded with a very appreciative audience, which had been singularly absent from his previous critical successes. For Jayne Mansfield, the role of the Hollywood sex symbol provided her first major exposure. Matthau's attention, however, was attracted by another pretty girl in the cast, one Carol Wellington-Smythe Marcus. Carol was employed as Jayne Mansfield's stand-in, and Matthau noticed the difference. One scene called for him to administer a pat to his leading lady's behind . . . and I discovered that whereas Jayne's rear was so hard I nearly cracked a finger on it, Carol's was soft and feminine. It's as good a reason as any for marriage, isn't it?', Matthau declared.

The couple's surprise discovery of each other blossomed and their marriage ceremony took place on 21 August 1959. Both had been married before – Carol to the writer William Saroyan, and Matthau to Grace Johnson with whom he had two children, David and Jennifer. Matthau has kept his first marriage a closed book but one can imagine how the insecurities of a young actor, coupled with a chronic desire to gamble, could have placed undue strain on any union. Intelligent, shrewd and outgoing Carol appears to have taken Matthau's worries in her stride and provided much needed security for him. Matthau is more direct in assessing their relationship: 'Carol and I are absolutely perfect for each other. She's crazy. I'm crazy. It's a very balanced relationship.'

His alimony and child maintenance payments contributed heftily to his poor financial shape and it was obvious from his gambling habit that he wasn't the most provident money manager. In 1955 he had appeared in two stage revivals – *The Wisteria Trees* and *Guys and Dolls* but the need for money was what prompted his entry into the world of films, another reason for marking 1955 as a turning point for him.

The first year of his film career brought two releases – *The Kentuckian* and *The Indian Fighter*. Up to now he had been rather contemptuous of 'the movies', reserving his interest and attention for stage work which he then considered to be of greater importance. With his expressive features and ability for characterisations it was a surprising attitude, since film work would have appeared to offer a natural showcase for his particular talents.

'I'm gonna cut that buckskin off you,' is hardly the most memorable first line in the history of the movies but it was not an untypical one in the context of most of the roles he would play as a supporting actor. One of only two films directed by Burt Lancaster, *The Kentuckian* was based on the novel *The Gabriel Horn* by Felix Holt and produced on location in Kentucky for Lancaster's own independent production company. An amiable, folksy drama, given added colour by its picturesque setting and authentic feel, it was a notch or two above the usual run-of-the-mill Western, but didn't have much success. Lancaster stars as a backwoodsman Eli Wakefield, intent on seeking the wide open spaces of Texas with his son, little Eli. Stopping en route, however, he is tempted by his cousin Zach (John McIntire) to adopt the life of a businessman and settle down with the local school-teacher Susie (Diana Lynn). Eventually, much to the relief of little Eli, Eli chooses the pioneering life.

Matthau plays Sam Bodine, the tavern-owner in the town of Humility and, from his very first encounter with Wakefield, a simmering rivalry develops between the two which erupts in a spectacular and bloody duel in which Wakefield is badly lashed by Bodine's whip before emerging triumphant. Wakefield gains something of an advantage from the intervention of Hanna (Dianne Foster), Bodine's serving girl, who rolls a wagon onto Bodine's whip.

When the film was first unveiled at the Venice Film Festival the bloody fight was met by cries of '*basta*' (enough), and in Britain the scene was cut by the censor before the film was passed for public exhibition.

A growling, smarmy villain, Matthau appears relaxed and confident before the cameras and in no way intimidated by the potent star quality of Lancaster. The character of Bodine is allowed the smallest measure of complexity – he too courts the schoolteacher and, on the appearance of the real villains of the film, two merciless brothers involved in a family feud with the Wakefields, he blanches at the prospect of cold-blooded murder and is killed for his reticence. But ultimately, Matthau's character lacks any real depth; Bodine is just a surly, ill-mannered bully who provides the opposition to good-guy Wakefield. Matthau was more blunt: 'A ridiculous part. . . . I did it because I was desperately short of money.'

He was a villain again in *The Indian Fighter*, the first production of Bryna, Kirk Douglas's own film company. It was shot in Oregon, and Douglas stars as Johnny Hawks who is sent from Fort Laramie to help a wagon train negotiate its way through Sioux Indian territory. Matthau is Wes Todd, the instigator of all the trouble between the Indians and the white men through his trading of whisky for gold. Hawks persuades Indian chief Red Cloud to sign a peace treaty in return for his promise to prevent the illegal bartering. When an Indian is killed, Red Wolf's brother, Grey Wolf, captures Todd, and Hawks fights for the right to take him back to face the justice of his own people. Todd tries to ingratiate himself with Hawks and shift the blame for the murder to his partner Chivington (Lon Chaney Jnr). Returning to Fort Laramie, Hawks ensures that both Todd and Chivington are jailed and sets off as guide and protector to the wagon train.

Todd and Chivington escape and find the goldmine, killing members of the Sioux tribe and breaking the peace treaty. The Indians retaliate by attacking the fort but Hawks brings Todd to Red Cloud and cements the peace by marrying the Chief's daughter Onahti (Elsa

Martinelli). Chivington has been killed in a mining explosion and Todd is also killed when he attempts to escape, thus ensuring that peace reigns supreme and that Hawks and Onahti live happily ever after. Although a routine Western, *The Indian Fighter* was directed by one-eyed André de Toth at a brisk clip.

Matthau was hardly enamoured by what the big screen had offered him so far, but was beginning to make the necessary adjustments from being a stage performer to working on the big screen. 'You have to work out the difference between the theatre and the cinema. When I first came to Hollywood I used to try and impress the people at the back of the camera and that was a mistake. You must half hide what you are wanting to show and make the audience feel that they are peeking in on what is happening. Audiences are like women. If you pursue them they'll retreat. You must hold back a little and let them come to you.'

After his film assignments he returned to *Will Success Spoil Rock Hunter?* and to the theatre where, like all good actors, he never stopped learning his craft. He was once asked what influence George Axelrod had had on his career. 'Maybe he taught me one or two things', Matthau replied. 'How not to act, for example. Maybe I taught him something: not to direct his own plays. Yes, there was an influence. I had the benefit of working with top-notch directors from George Abbott to Elia Kazan. That is the way to acquire your technical skill.'

He took an extended leave of absence from the long-running *Will Success Spoil Rock Hunter?* to return to the film capital for a more interesting assignment in *Bigger Than Life*, a controversial production, starring James Mason who was also the film's producer. Mason was then at the peak of his career, with *Bigger Than Life* following close on the heels of two of his biggest hits – *A Star is Born* and *20,000 Leagues Under the Sea*. Determined to produce something himself, he had read an article, entitled 'Ten Feet Tall', in the *New Yorker* magazine in the section 'Annals of Medicine' which recounts details of interesting medical cases. Deciding that there was material here for a film, Nicholas Ray, fresh from *Rebel Without a Cause*, was signed as the director.

Mason ensured that the filming took place in some secrecy; the set was closed to outsiders for the entire duration of the production and the last fifteen pages of script were not to be released until the final day of shooting. The fact is that the final section of the script probably wasn't ready until the final day of shooting, as the script proved an unusually flexible document. The usual filmmaking procedure is to have a completed script before production begins. During *Bigger Than Life* Nicholas Ray would often appear on set with amendments and new scenes that had been written the previous evening with help from his friend Clifford Odets and the British critic Gavin Lambert whose work on the film went uncredited.

Mason plays Ed Avery, a schoolteacher who supplements his income by working for a local cab company. One day he collapses and is rushed to hospital where he is prescribed a course of the drug cortisone, which alleviates the pain but has unwelcome side-effects on his personality. Under the influence of the drug Ed becomes argumentative and dictatorial. He has been exceeding the stated dose and begins to fake prescriptions to gain an extra supply of the drug. Ed becomes prey to fits of temper and displays a cruel, sadistic streak. Frightened by the change in his father, Ed's son Richie (Christopher Olsen) attempts to steal and destroy his father's medicine but he is discovered whereupon Ed announces that he intends to kill Richie, his wife Lou

(Barbara Rush) and then himself. Lou calls a family friend, Wally (Matthau), a close colleague at Ed's school, and he arrives in time to restrain Ed forcibly and see that he gains proper medical attention. Treated for his addiction, Ed is ready to face the future with his family and friends.

On the film's release, Twentieth Century-Fox played up the sensationalistic aspects of the story with the advertising slogan, 'A motion picture so shocking you must ask how did they dare make it?' The film was shown, to a favourable response, at the Venice Film Festival but received a rough ride from the majority of critics on both sides of the Atlantic. In Britain a special screening for the medical profession had been arranged prior to the film's opening. The medical men were outraged at the film's treatment of the 'wonder drug' cortisone and said that the film was 'disgraceful and distorting' and 'dangerous nonsense'. They claimed that cortisone was non-addictive and that the film could damage public confidence in a drug beneficial in the treatment of arthritis and rheumatics. Fox were asked to withdraw the film. Mason countered that the film was based on a true incident, and made the following statement: 'I have tried to portray dramatically the evils of an indiscriminate use of drugs. I should be aided and applauded by the drug industry.' The medical men retaliated that the original American patient had had a previous history of psychosis. Either way, the argument created little audience interest. In America *Time* magazine compared the film to, 'a peep show seen in a padded cell'.

A disappointed Mason put the film's failure down to several factors: it was ahead of its time, a quasi-documentary approach would have been better realised had they filmed in black and white, and audiences were

33

unwilling to accept Mason as an average American schoolteacher. It's a shame because the film is a powerful melodrama featuring a strong performance by Mason and an unusually sympathetic role for the novice Matthau. Certainly press releases of the time stated that Matthau considered the part the most important in his fledgeing film career. Perhaps, had it been more successful, it might have opened doors to a wider range of supporting roles for the immediate future.

When the filming of *Bigger Than Life* was completed (with a visit from Marilyn Monroe – the one exception to the no visitors rule) Matthau returned East to play out his role in *Will Success Spoil Rock Hunter?* He was probably relieved to escape the perils of California driving. On arriving in Hollywood he had rented a car to drive between his apartment and the studio. Within four weeks he had been involved in three separate accidents, none of which had been his fault. On each occasion the police had recorded that Matthau 'observed the vehicle code and was in complete control of his car'. In each incident a local driver had violated the law.

At this point in his career Matthau could be said to be building slowly but surely towards some kind of status within his profession. Certainly in terms of the size of his billing and the number of lines assigned to his characters which was increasing, and this is one crude measure of achievement. He was much in demand for a variable list of credits, but he can't have considered himself star material. He hadn't as yet been given the opportunity to shine in a good role and make it his own in the public's eye; he had no gimmick for which anyone clamoured, didn't appear to have found a particular niche to call his own. He was a solidly professional performer with any number of talents that could bubble to the surface in the right role, but what he lacked was a 'star-making' role. It would be a long time coming.

Interestingly enough, his first three films all reflect the shift in power that was taking place in film-making, a shift that would eventually be to his benefit. The era of the independent actor-producer, running his own company and making his own career decisions, provided the base which would undermine the dominance, good or bad, long held by the major studios and the contract system. Both Burt Lancaster and Kirk Douglas owned the companies which produced *The Kentuckian* and *The Indian Fighter*. Under the old system, of grooming photogenic personalities for stardom, of protecting images, of shortlived starlets and beefcake, it is entirely possible that Matthau would never have become a film star – he didn't have the looks, the posture or the potential under the movie-making rules which had once applied and the vestiges of which were still pertinent in the fifties. The shake-up of that system, then in progress, allowed an unconventional star like Matthau to break through because, quite simply, he had talent. That, however, was in the future – the Walter Matthau of 1957 needed to work to pay the bills and be able to take a flutter on a promising filly.

Matthau was seen in two films released during 1957, the more interesting of which is undoubtedly *A Face in the Crowd*, a second collaboration between writer Budd Schulberg and director Elia Kazan, both Oscar winners for 1954's *On the Waterfront*.

In *A Face in the Crowd*, Patricia Neal stars as a roving reporter for 'the best radio programme in North East Arkansas', with the motto that 'people are fascinatin' wherever you find them'. One of the most fascinatin' turns out to be Lonesome Larry Rhodes (Andy Griffith) who features on the programme from the local jail. His brief moment, singing a song and offering crackerbarrel asides, generates such a strong audience reaction that he is given a permanent radio spot. An uncouth, and ultimately unscrupulous, hickster with a simple 'country boy' character, Lonesome gains enormous appeal from his direct approach to the common people and his affinity with the masses. He learns the power of his popularity when he is able publicly to humiliate a sheriff running for office.

'Lonesome' moves on to the more lucrative pickings of television in Memphis with his benefactor (Neal) in tow. Bowled over by the man's definite attraction, Neal is able to smooth his rougher edges and generally manages his demands. In Memphis she meets Mel Miller (Matthau), an easy-going, college-educated television manager who will become a spectator to the rise and fall of 'Lonesome' Rhodes.

Eventually Rhodes graduates to national television and nationwide stardom as the beloved Will Rogers of the small screen – a true man of the people. In reality, he is self-seeking and egotistical with a well-developed disgust for the gullibility of his sixty-five-million audience.

Mel departs the 'Lonesome' circus and regains his self-respect as a serious writer. He meets up again with the Neal character in New York armed with a copy of his forthcoming book, *Demigog in Denim*, which unmasks 'Lonesome' as a fraud. Neal has herself become increasingly disillusioned with 'Lonesome' who constantly takes her for granted and has reneged on a promise to marry her, choosing instead the pert charms of champion batton-twirler Lee Remick. And so she decides to destroy her creation by leaving a mike on at the end of a show allowing 'Lonesome's' insulting comments about the mentality of his audience to be broadcast to the nation. Exorcised of her demon she can face the future with Mel.

Based on Schulberg's short story, 'Our Arkansas Traveller', *A Face in the Crowd* remains a powerful drama of the competitive power of the media and the abuse of celebrity. Matthau's character, the educated Mel Miller, the object of 'Lonesome's' ridicule, is believed to be a self-portrait by Schulberg. Decked out with glasses and pipe, Matthau bears those traditional hallmarks of the intellectual with some skill. Miller, a 1944 graduate of Nashville, has an educated openness that contrasts strongly with the instinctive cunning of Andy Griffith's 'Lonesome'. Matthau develops the shadings of tolerant, world-weary cynicism into a sympathetic portrait. The fact that Miller takes a stand by leaving his well-paid cocoon of employment with Lonesome strengthens audience empathy with the character. In the role Matthau even brings off a characteristic bit business with a lunging perusal of a hotel corridor in the manner of Groucho Marx. His definition of a character through a walk has become a noted facet of his technique.

Unfortunately, the see-sawing nature of Matthau's film career plunged downwards with *Slaughter on Tenth Avenue*. In this film Richard Egan plays deputy district attorney William Keating who masterminds 'one of the greatest law enforcement victories in the violent and almost savage waterfront of New York'. Investigating the murder of a stevedore he gains the confidence of the dockers and undermines the rackets of waterfront boss Al Dahlke. Matthau plays Dahlke, described as 'the cold-blooded Czar of Manhattan's waterfront'.

Egan was the star again in the following year's *Voice in the Mirror*. In this film Matthau slipped down the cast list as Leon Karnes, a doctor attempting to help alcoholic Jim Burton (Egan) to keep off the drink. Told in flashback, the film is a downmarket variation of *Lost Weekend*, with Egan disregarding the good doctor's advice and going his own way to cure his problem, through the formation of a self-help, mini Alcoholics Anonymous. Ten years on and the sober Burton finds that his unorthodox methods have helped many to conquer the lure of the bottle.

Both competent if little seen dramas, Matthau places them squarely in an uninteresting period of, 'more lousy movies than I care to remember'.

He remained on the wrong side of the law the same year in the Elvis Presley vehicle *King Creole*. Based on Harold Robbins' novel *A Stone for Danny Fisher*, *King Creole* was Presley's first opportunity to display any dramatic worth and Presley himself believed; 'For the first time in my screen career I'm playing somebody other than Elvis Presley.' The film was directed by veteran Hollywood craftsman Michael Curtiz, responsible in his time for *The Adventures of Robin Hood* (1938), *Yankee Doodle Dandy* (1942), *Casablanca* (1943) and *Mildred Pierce* (1945).

Presley stars as Danny Fisher, a New Orleans kid who lives with his father and sister. He works at a nightclub to supplement the family income and hopes to graduate from high school. However, he is soon led astray by the charms of Ronnie (Carolyn Jones) who works at the Blue Shade nightclub run by racketeer Maxie Fields (Matthau). Maxie owns most of Bourbon Street. Fisher also becomes involved with a gang of hoodlums and turns to crime. However, he can also sing and his vocal talents earn him a job at a rival nightclub as well as ensuring that he stays out of the hands of the police. His success at the rival nightclub, the King Creole, draws away all the patrons from Maxie's Blue Shade.

Maxie exacts his revenge but Danny, troubled by an attack on his father, proves in a climactic brawl that right will prevail.

Matthau's Maxie Fields is perhaps his definitive study

of a rich, ruthless racketeer and, although he is alleged to have joked with Presley that if he would only try singing some Sinatra-style ballads he'd be much more popular, he had some words of praise for him in later years; 'A very modest man. But then he must have been to perform the way he did. Actually, I'm kidding. Considering he had no training at all, he was remarkably good.' *King Creole* was undoubtedly one of Presley's best dramatic vehicles.

Ride a Crooked Trail, also a 1958 release, was an assembly-line Audie Murphy Western that found Matthau squarely on the side of law and order, as Judge Kyle, and officer of the law in Little Rock. Murphy plays outlaw Joe Maybe who rides into town with his sights set on the contents of the local bank. He has assumed the identity of lawman Marshal Jim Noonan, and Kyle places him in charge of keeping the peace. It's a responsibility that forces Joe to turn honest, arresting Sam Teeler (Henry Silva) and his gang and thus earning the judge's approval and the right to wear his marshal's badge.

Matthau's fourth 1958 release, his most productive year as a supporting actor, was a rare early comedy – *Onionhead*, with Andy Griffith. Griffith plays Al Woods who joins the US Coast Guard service after a quarrel with his college sweetheart Jo (Erin O'Brien). He is assigned to the USS *Periwinkle* off Boston as a ship's cook, third class. In Boston he meets Stella (Felicia Farr) and believes 'this is love'. Life on board the *Periwinkle* is soured by the grouchy chief cook Red Wildoe (Matthau) who is critical of everything Al does. Red even dates Stella and the two are married with Red being transferred and Al promoted to chief cook. The path of true love may not run smooth but Al and Jo are eventually reunited after he has proved his worth as a cook and a sailor.

Onionhead had been designed as a follow-up to Griffith's army comedy, *No Time for Sergeants* (1958), using similar antics with a change of service to freshen the story. Largely slapstick in nature, *Onionhead* gains laughs from incidents like the one in which Griffith overloads the yeast in the ship's bread mixture, with predictable results. Griffith was the star but Matthau's first comic film role allows him to brighten the proceedings as the demanding, testy, tippling cook, described by one writer as an 'irresistibly funny performance'.

After his lucrative foray into movies he returned to New York and a Broadway play, *Once More With Feeling* by Harry Kurnitz, a comedy concerning the strained relations between a musical conductor and his wife. Matthau's supporting performance as a harassed and harried go-between enlivened the film and won him a second New York Drama Critics Award, restoring some of the confidence which he must have lacked from most of his screen roles.

When he wasn't gambling away his earnings he was in a fairly healthy financial position and managed to persuade his mother to move from her New York tenement. The incident provoked one of his many stories about her: 'I got my mother out of a tenement in New York and down to Florida. Now my mother has a habit of stealing toilet paper from cafeterias. She goes into a cafeteria, has a cup of coffee, goes to the john and steals the toilet paper. By the time she moved, she had ten or fifteen brown paper bags full. I got very angry, I said, mom, this is a new apartment, I don't want you stealing toilet paper, go out and buy some. And I took the bags and emptied the toilet paper into the bath and turned on the tap. She grabbed me – we had a terrific fight. She said, 'You're crazy, you're an actor, I don't know, I guess I brought you up wrong.' I said, 'Mom, I'm going for a walk – I'll be back in an hour.' I came back to the apartment and went out on the terrace and there, spread all over the floor of the terrace, she had the individual sheets of toilet paper – drying!'

As a performer he had never been busier – films in Hollywood, plays in New York, television whenever and wherever he could; the public may still not have known the name but his face was unavoidable. Later he would say, 'The problem is that I'm too good. I don't look like an actor. I could be anyone from a toilet attendant to a business executive. People either ask me, "Are you a television actor?", or else, "Are you from Erie, Pa?".'

And that was the problem in *Will Success Spoil Rock Hunter?* He convinced audiences that he was a struggling young playwright; in *Onionhead* the audience couldn't believe him to be anything other than a bad-tempered cook with a fondness for drink. Each creation convinced and entertained within its own setting but there was no crossover from one role to another that would allow the public to build up an image of Walter Matthau or indeed build up an expectation of what a Matthau performance would deliver. Whilst it denied him the opportunity of playing the lead, it did allow him the luxury of not being branded with any persona or filed in any restrictive pigeonhole. He could play any nationality, portray any shade of immorality and crookedness, be comic or sinister and the only drawback was that he wasn't a star.

He did gain the lead role in *Tallahassee 7000*, a forgettable television series. He played Lex Rogers, special agent, troubleshooter for the Florida Sheriff's Bureau based at Miami Beach. The title for this crime series stemmed from the Bureau phone number, Tallahassee 7000, and some thirty-nine half-hour episodes were filmed which were eventually syndicated during the 1961 season.

This was also the period which saw the peak of his gambling fever – whether his addiction was a sign of his insecurity, a by-product of his youth or an 'escape valve' from his career worries only he can really say, but in the late fifties it was crippling. 'The worst moment I recall was back in 1958, when I was doing a television series. I bet $20,000 on the Yankees and they lost. I bet $80,000 on their second game and they lost one nil. I went out and had a Scotch in Goldman's bar across the street. Well eighteen Scotches. I'd lost $100,000. I wasn't drunk, just petrified. I walked out into the sun, feeling like a piece of cardboard.'

Even an experience like that didn't make him stop, neither did his marriage to the remarkably understanding Carol in 1959. The couple worked together on a film that year, *Gangster Story*, which was released in December. Matthau also directed the film, 'presumably on a dare' wrote one critic. Tracing the rise and fall of a vicious 'one-man criminal genius', Jack Martin (Matthau), *Gangster Story* was an all-action relative of the recently successful *Al Capone* starring Rod Steiger. Martin eventually joins forces with a local kingpin Earl Dawson (Bruce McFarlan) and his gang for a bank raid, but they are all killed in a shoot-out with the police. Carol (Carol Grace/Matthau), the local librarian that Martin had been romancing, learns of the news on her car radio whilst driving to Mexico.

Hardly the most promising material, and the title song 'The Itch for the Scratch' can't have helped matters. Nevertheless the *Hollywood Reporter* rated the film as 'good' and outlined the financial prospects thus: 'Judging from past market reactions to Al Capone et al, it's apparent that *Gangster Story* will draw an encouraging quantity of patrons in the type of theatre for which it is destined. Paul Purcell's hard-ringing screenplay has stressed a minimum of characterisation study and a maximum of fast-flowing action, a combination that spells box-office.' The independent production, however, received few bookings and was not the kind of success envisaged by the *Hollywood Reporter*. Matthau has never expressed any desire to direct again although in TV Movies, Leonard Maltin heralds the film as a 'straightforward, tight little gangster chronicle'.

His seesaw career was on a downer which continued through a flop of a play, *Once There Was a Russian*, and a worthless role in the film *Strangers When We Meet* (1960), a production of Kirk Douglas's company Bryna from the bestselling Evan Hunter book. A tale of suburban adultery in the same mould as *Peyton Place*, *Strangers When We Meet* features Douglas as idealistic architect and family man Larry Coe who falls in love with his beautiful neighbour Margaret Gault (Kim Novak), unhappily married and also seeking some extra-marital interests.

Whilst working on a mountain-top house for writer Roger Altar (Ernie Kovacs) Larry and Margaret meet more often and embark on a clandestine affair. Larry's wife Eve (Barbara Rush) hosts a house party; among the guests are Felix Anders (Matthau) and his wife Betty (Helen Gallagher), another unhappy couple. At the party Felix drops broad hints to Larry about the many opportunities to 'play around'.

When Larry is offered a 'dream opportunity' to build a city in Hawaii, he asks Margaret to bring their love into the open and start afresh, but he has obviously been more serious about their affair than she has. When Larry returns home he discovers that Felix has paid a call to try his luck with the neglected Eve. Eve has rejected his advances but Larry is enraged, chases after Felix and knocks him into the gutter. Felix demands: 'Tell me how I'm any different from you.' Larry chews on this and is reconciled with Eve as the two decide to leave for Hawaii.

The film's director, Richard Quine, generally a comedy specialist, ordered the unusual step of actually building a house in Bel Air to give an authentic background to the work of Kirk Douglas's architect in the film. Quine also managed to keep the finished house once the filming was over. A glossy soap-opera, *Strangers When We Meet* saddles Matthau with another thankless character, described as, 'the neighbourhood wolf lecherously on the prowl for dispirited wives'. Matthau plays him as a breezy, pipe-smoking opportunist.

If his presence was noted at all in this series of film roles the reaction was generally favourable, although it must have been galling for an actor of almost fifteen years' experience to find himself named as Walter Mathieu in the *Saturday Review*.

Television at least offered him variety and the early sixties saw him tackle the role of Captain Jack Boyle in Sean O'Casey's *Juno and the Paycock* with Hume Cronyn as Joxer Daly; and, for contrast, an ostentatiously *nouveau-riche* gangster in an episode of the now badly-dated series *The Naked City* entitled 'The Man Who Bit the Diamond in Half'.

The period of *Gangster Story* and *Strangers When We Meet* marked something of a regression in his career after his stage success in *Once More With Feeling* and good film roles in *Bigger Than Life*, *A Face in the Crowd*, *King Creole* and *Onionhead*. The advance that might have been expected to take place hadn't materialised and he still lacked that one crystallising part which would establish him as a star. There were consolations in the awards, the good reviews and the respect in which he was held by his peers but, at the age of forty, he must have despaired of ever becoming a bankable star. Some stars were already past their peak at this age, while he was still scrambling around to pay the bills and had only a handful of roles he could point to with any sense of pride or accomplishment.

Nevertheless, in the half-dozen years since *Will Success Spoil Rock Hunter?* he had begun to acquire a following and a reputation, although real success still eluded him. In his private life, his mother was well taken care of, toilet paper and all, and his marriage to Carol was some kind of stabilising influence in his life. He was still a risk-taking gambler, it was a habit he would never break with entirely, but his expensive binge in 1958 would stand as the nadir of his recklessness. In his career, however erratically it was developing, there was always a welcome for his characterisations and, in the right role, there was a warm audience response. He was a talented all-round actor, all he needed to reach the top were the right breaks and, after a long haul, the tide was about to turn in his favour.

Chapter Four

Matthau can trace the beginning of his rise to stardom back to 1962 and a Broadway play called *A Shot in the Dark* with Julie Harris. A fast-moving farce in which a woman is accused of shooting her lover, *A Shot in the Dark* eventually formed the basis of the second Peter Sellers-Blake Edwards *Inspector Clouseau* comedy. Matthau entered the stage production during the try-outs in Kentucky when a fellow actor died and a quick replacement was called for. The play was a hit and Matthau's haughty French aristocrat won him the prestigious Tony Award as the year's best supporting actor. The character gave him a chance to perfect one of his famous walks. 'I've used a lot of different walks. I was doing a play in a drama class and the teacher said to me, "You walk like you are going to the Automat. You are a duke! You must come out and smell the people." I always remembered that. I used it in *A Shot in the Dark*. I walked out like my mother walks when she has to go to the bathroom and I stood looking into the audience and sniffed. They got it right away.'

He also had decent roles in two 1962 film releases – *Lonely Are The Brave* and *Who's Got the Action*? Matthau's work in *Lonely Are The Brave* marked his third association with a Kirk Douglas production. Douglas, in one of his favourite roles, plays a loner cowboy, Jack Burns, a man out of step with the contemporary age. Visiting Albuquerque he instigates a saloon brawl to force his arrest and thus allow him to help his friend Paul Bondi (Michael Kane) escape from prison. Paul has been arrested for helping to smuggle Mexicans across the border but agrees with his wife Jerri (Gena Rowlands) that it's better for everyone if he serves his sentence. Jack however, as a man of the open spaces, refuses to be held in captivity and breaks loose from the jail, heading for the hills. His allies are his horse and his gun. It falls to the reluctant Sheriff Johnson (Matthau) to track down the fugitive with radio links and a helicopter to assist him. The fugitive initially makes good his escape, but trying to cross a highway by night both horse and rider are struck down by a diesel truck.

Lonely Are The Brave is a protest against the urbanisation and mechanisation of contemporary society and Douglas was drawn to the role of a bemused individual in a world of conformity. 'It happens to be a point of view I love', Douglas has said. 'This is what attracted me to the story – the difficulty of being an individual today. Life gets more and more complex and convoluted. Young people are not happy with what's going on – and they're right. The character in *Lonely Are The Brave* had that quality. He didn't want to belong to this day and age. It's difficult to buck the system. That's the tragedy of it all.'

Matthau is the representative of order in the new civilisation that no longer has a place for Douglas's rebellious cowboy. Although he is appreciative of the fugitive's desire to live by his own code, Matthau's Sheriff Johnson is duty-bound to pursue the man and bring him to justice. Humane and sympathetic, Johnson realises that, for all his reservations, the law has been broken and that he has a job to do. In America journalist

Pauline Kael described his performance as 'ingenious and entertaining', while in Britain his work was applauded for presenting 'a cynic of immensely world-weary character'. He was honoured for the first time as a film actor with the *Film Daily* award for *Lonely Are The Brave*.

In contrast *Who's Got the Action?*, made in the same year, was pure candyfloss. The plot centres on writer Melanie Flood (Lana Turner), who is distraught over her husband's gambling losses – $8000 in the previous eight months, and is considering divorce. Her husband Steve (Dean Martin) is a lawyer and Melanie involves his partner Clint (Eddie Albert) in what she thinks is the perfect solution to her problem; unknown to Steve she will act as his bookie and keep the losses in the family. Steve is won over to this mystery bookie and places $100 on a seventeen-to-one longshot – Blue Eyes. The horse wins and Melanie has to come up with his winnings.

Steve interests another three cronies in his new bookie and Melanie has to turn to her neighbour, nightclub singer Saturday Knight (Nita Talbot) for help. Saturday buys her household artefacts and jewellery and thus gains the admiration of her marriage-shy boyfriend Tony Gagoots (Matthau) for her new-found taste. Gagoots is the penny-pinching head of the local rackets, preoccupied by the loss of four high revenue customers from his computer system. Eventually, when Melanie is faced with the possibility of paying out $18,000 if a sixty-to-one 'creaky old zombie' wins, all is revealed. Steve blackmails Gagoots to cover any debts by convincing him that Saturday will divulge his many business secrets unless he pays up. This act prompts the gangster to marry Saturday, as a wife can't testify against her husband. Steve and Melanie are happily reunited and Gagoots tells them that the moral of this episode is 'not to play with crazy independents. Stick to an old established firm.'

Who's Got the Action? is diverting froth with attractive stars and enough sharp lines to satisfy an audience in search of pure entertainment. Lana Turner appears in eighteen different outfits especially created by Edith Head and is the kind of chipper writer who can say, 'I just have time to finish a chapter before I run down for the results.' Matthau and Talbot have the most colourful roles and they generally manage to upstage the assured comic touch of the stars. Talbot's Saturday Knight extracts the most from her relationship with the understandably retiring Gagoots, commenting, 'He's the romantic type – never phones up himself in case I'm recording it. Everything's done through a middle man, well, almost everything.' Matthau's mother-fixated mobster running a computerised business is a clever comic creation that runs away with the film whenever he appears. 'Are you familiar with the statute on breaking and entry?' enquires Dean Martin, playing the straight man. 'From childhood,' bellows Matthau. A milk-drinking, apple-crunching mobster, Tony Gagoots is described as 'looking like Mack the Knife on a bad day'. Matthau rampages through the part like some scene-stealing moose and arrests audience attention.

Who's Got the Action? marked the first solo film for writer-producer Jack Rose. A former radio writer for Bob Hope, Rose, in partnership with Mel Shavelson, had been responsible for films like *Houseboat* (1958) with Cary Grant and Sophia Loren as well as the Danny Kaye vehicles *The Five Pennies* (1959) and *On the Double* (1961). A publicity hand-out for the film claimed, 'Producer Jack Rose feels fortunate in talking Matthau into taking the part, since the actor is first and foremost a legitimate theatre performer, taking only film roles which he feels are worth doing.' Considering Matthau's own justification for some of his early film appearances that statement can be taken with a pinch of salt. None the less, *Who's Got the Action?* was an attractive shop window for his talents and he received better reviews than anyone else in the film. Over the next few years the critics were uniformly on his side, applauding him, regardless of the quality of his films, and cheering him on to the top.

Matthau had taken a leave of absence from *A Shot in the Dark* to appear in the film and couldn't afford to be out of work for any length of time. He was offered a role in the Doris Day comedy *The Thrill of It All* by producer Ross Hunter but was passed over in favour of Edward Andrews when he demanded a fee of $100,000. Matthau claimed it was a lousy role anyway and wasn't worth $10,000. In the past few years he had been making $150,000 a year on average but it soon disappeared, with ten per cent going to his agent, ten per cent to his business manager and $60,000 a year in alimony and child support payments. In 1963, Carol gave birth to a son, Charlie, providing another demand on his father's income, which was still under attack from Matthau's gambling habit. The antics of Lana Turner in *Who's Got the Action?* must have struck a responsive chord in Carol.

In 1963 he enlivened *Island of Love* as Greek gangster Tony Dallas involved in the misfiring con-man schemes of Steve Blair (Robert Preston). Dallas is persuaded to invest two million dollars in Blair's film *Genesis*, the story of Adam and Eve, on condition that his girlfriend Cha Cha (Betty Bruce) is cast as Eve. Cha Cha is allergic to apples and can't act. The film is a flop and Dallas wants his money back. Blair and his partner Paul Ferris (Tony Randall) escape to Greece and perpetrate another con planting fake antiquities. Blair turns the island of

Paradeisos into an 'Island of Love'. However, Dallas is on his trail but relents when he finds Blair has become engaged to his niece Elena (Georgia Moll) who lives on the island. A well-photographed travelogue, *Island of Love* was a fairly pallid comedy.

Soon after this spell of filming in Greece, Matthau was back in Europe for the location shooting of *Charade* in France. Filmed in and around Paris, *Charade* took in such famous landmarks as Les Halles, Notre Dame, the colonnades of the Palais Royal and the Metro. It is a sleek, elegant Hitchcock-style thriller with an immensely convoluted plot put over with charm by top stars Cary Grant and Audrey Hepburn. To simplify the plot, the story goes as follows: Hepburn is Regina 'Reggie' Lambert who returns home from a skiing holiday to discover her estranged husband has been murdered and their apartment stripped of all furniture, paintings and clothes. The police explain that her husband had auctioned their possessions for $250,000 but the money is nowhere to be found. Reggie is suddenly much in demand; from the suspicious Adam Canfield (Cary Grant) who is really a Treasury official, from outright villains Gideon, Scobie and Tex (Ned Glass, George Kennedy and James Coburn) and from the truly treacherous Hamilton Bartholomew (Matthau) who claims to be the Head of the CIA but is really Carson Dyle, a vengeance-seeking wartime veteran. Eventually it transpires that Reggie is in possession of stamps worth $250,000. In a tense chase that spills over on to the stage of the Comédie Française, Adam saves her by opening a trapdoor through which Bartholomew/Dyle plunges to his death.

Matthau is seen to good advantage as the seemingly trustworthy CIA chief and takes part in the exciting 'set piece' chase through the columns of the Palais Royal where the Givenchy-clad Hepburn is torn between

Grant and Matthau, either one of which could prove a threat to her life. *Charade* has style, confidence, polish and a glossy Henry Mancini score. A popular film, it was the number four attraction in America throughout 1964 with domestic rentals in excess of six million dollars.

Matthau capitalised on his growing movie fame in 1964 with a trio of productions that offered conclusive proof of his versatility. In *Ensign Pulver* he was the worldly-wise ship's doctor, in *Goodbye Charlie* he contributed an outrageously entertaining portrait of a Hungarian film producer, and in the chilling *Fail Safe* he was a coolly calculating civilian hawk. He received an excellent set of reviews and stole the show completely in *Goodbye Charlie*.

Ensign Pulver was a weak follow-on to *Mister Roberts*, lacking not only the original cast but any semblance of wit or invention. Robert Walker Jnr took over the role which won an Oscar for Jack Lemmon and Matthau inherited the part first played by William Powell in his final screen appearance. The film was generally villified by the press but Matthau escaped the free-flying wrath as can be witnessed in this *Playboy* review: 'Robert Walker, as Pulver, resembles his late father in everything but talent. Burl Ives (the Captain) is a fat bad actor – or, if you prefer, a bad fat actor. Walter Matthau (Doc) is a good actor waiting for a decent part.'

Sir Leopold Sartori in the film version of George Axelrod's *Goodbye Charlie* was a plum role. A rather tasteless farce which had been a stage hit for Lauren Bacall, *Goodbye Charlie* is about a womanising wastrel, shot while escaping through a port-hole, being re-incarnated as a woman. Debbie Reynolds gamely attempted the role of Charlie (once intended for Marilyn Monroe) and the incomparable comic skills of Tony Curtis were on hand as Charlie's best friend George who copes with a host of complications before the demise of the second Charlie. Matthau is the Hungarian Leopold Sartori, a film producer with an eye for the ladies. A cigar-smoking, Alexander Korda-style mogul, surrounded by sycophancy, Sartori seems to have a patent on insincerity. George says of him: 'Compared to you Charlie was Francis of Assissi', to which Sartori retorts, 'If I were not Hungarian by birth I would be speechless.' It is aboard Sartori's yacht, the Aphrodite, that he shoots Charlie and starts the twisted chain of events. He is surprised by all the fuss: 'I shoot one little writer,' he pleads. Played with a goulash-thick accent and an over-the-top range of expressions and gesticulations, Matthau invests the character with enough life to keep the film afloat. In Britain Dilys Powell of the *Sunday Times* noted, 'only Walter Matthau, prowling like some mischievous puma through the Hollywood upholstery brings life with a giant caricature of a European impressario'.

Fail Safe was rather overshadowed, coming as it did in the wake of *Dr Strangelove* (1964), but presents a sobering doomsday warning of the latitude of error in the nuclear age. In the film a mechanical malfunction has ordered the American air force to drop two twenty-megaton bombs on Moscow. The Americans are unable to countermand the order because the Russians are jamming their radio signals.

The American President (Henry Fonda) contacts his opposite number in Russia and attempts to persuade him of the misunderstanding. Eventually the President sends American bombers to destroy his own planes and helps the Russian fighters towards the same end. He seeks the advice of his closest aides including civilian adviser Groeteschele (Matthau) who believes that this is a golden opportunity to stage an all-out nuclear attack which will destroy the communist threat once and for all. The President disregards the lunacy of his opinions and when Moscow is destroyed he orders his own men to carry out the same attack on New York. With this act, an uneasy trust is re-established.

Fail Safe began as a project of a former United Artists executive Max Youngstein, the first from his independent production set-up based in New York. The film's director, Sidney Lumet, told a *Newsday* interviewer: 'We're suddenly living with things that are out of control. All of a sudden we're helpless. We can't do anything. There ain't no answers. The machines are big; they're bigger than we are . . . Well, I'm not going to leave it to an IBM machine whether I'm going to be blown sky-high or not, not if I can help it.'

Fail Safe was filming in New York at the same time as Stanley Kubrick's black comedy about nuclear war, *Dr Strangelove*, was being made in England. The studio releasing *Dr Strangelove* purchased the rights to *Fail Safe* and delayed its release. Despite a prestigious opening at the New York Film Festival *Fail Safe* did not fare well commercially. Lumet commented, 'I didn't know anything about *Strangelove* until we'd finished shooting and were sued . . . I knew we were dead as a movie as soon as Columbia bought us, because I knew they had done that to hold us off until *Dr Strangelove* was released.

Matthau's Groeteschele is a cold, Kissinger-like darling of the social set who are amused by his theories that a sacrifice of sixty million lives is necessary to win a nuclear war. His philosophy is that of the survival of the fittest without the luxury of moral dilemma. A civilian war-mongerer and sardonic monomaniac, it is a characterisation in rich contrast to his comic roles of the same year. The film finally appeared in Britain during 1965 when the noted critic Kenneth Tynan wrote, 'The leading hawk is a civilian (played by Walter Matthau, conceivably the best character actor in America).'

1965 saw the release of only one Matthau film because by that time he was gainfully employed on the stage. The film was *Mirage*, a mystery starring Gregory Peck, where once again Matthau was the best reason for parting with the admission money.

Peck, as David Stillman, spends most of the film wandering around in a daze, understandably so since he is suffering from amnesia. Stillman finds himself at the Unidyne Building in New York during a power cut, unable to recall the events of the past two years. He is being followed by a man with a gun but doesn't remember why. He seeks a psychiatrist's help but is unable to convince Dr Broden (Robert Harris) that he is not a fugitive from justice. He then approaches the AAA Detective Agency and enlists the services of the inexperienced Ted Caselle (Matthau). They begin to unravel the mystery but back at the Unidyne Building they are accosted by a hired thug, Willard (George Kennedy). The two men split up and agree to meet later, but when Stillman arrives at the detective's office he finds Caselle murdered. Eventually Stillman finds the key to his past as an employee at Garrison Laboratories in California where he had discovered a formula for eliminating radioactive fallout from nuclear weapons. His employer Charles Calvin (Walter Abel) has bitterly disillusioned him by pointing out the commercial value of such a discovery to his business partner Crawford (Leif Erickson). In New York Stillman had set light to his formula and tossed it· out the window with Calvin plunging to his death in an attempt to save the document. The shock of Calvin's death has triggered Stillman's amnesia. He realises that Crawford and his associates have been pursuing him to hush up the incident and discover the formula. Returning to Dr Broden for psychiatric help Stillman's memory is completely restored and he triumphs over the villains.

The plot is a very busy one and in later years Peck claimed, 'I forget what the hell it was all about'. He also said, 'I think my main contribution to the film was that I hired Walter.' Peck had seen Matthau on stage and judged him good value for money at $75,000 for the supporting role. Matthau was again singled out for praise by reviewers. *Time* magazine observed: 'Scenarist Peter Stone (*Charade*) varies the pace with droll asides, most of them knowingly shrugged off by Matthau as the reluctant snoop who abhors firearms and acts of heroism, and struggles gamely to look hard-bitten while guzzling Dr Pepper!'

The stage work that kept Matthau off screen during this period was something special – *The Odd Couple*, described by Matthau as, 'That situation which comes once in a lifetime when the actor and the part blend just right.' It was also the second and conclusive turning point in his professional fortunes. Matthau and playwright Neil Simon had met at a cocktail party a couple of years before when Simon had the beginning of a new play that he had written specially for the actor. Simon, a retiring, donnish figure, nicknamed 'Doc', was born in the Bronx and credits part of his immense success to a misspent youth at the movies; at the age of eight he was forcibly ejected from one theatre for laughing hysterically at Chaplin's *Modern Times*. After a career writing comedy material for radio and television he had arrived on Broadway with his 1961 hit *Come Blow Your Horn* and had already followed this with a second hit, *Barefoot in the Park*.

Matthau has recalled their first meeting: 'He came up to me at a party one night and pushed two acts of a play into my hands saying, "I've written this for you". I didn't know who the hell he was. But I read it and at first it looked like one long string of gags. Then I reckoned I saw a spine in it and that it could work. We took it out on the road and Neil Simon wanted to polish up every line which didn't get a laugh. But we pleaded with him to let most of them stay in so that we didn't push the audience too hard and we could give them a story. That was *The Odd Couple*.'

It is well known that there is a strong element of autobiography in all of Simon's best work and the events and characters in *The Odd Couple* are based on a period in the life of Simon's elder brother Danny. '*The Odd Couple* was based on a true incident with living people, my brother and Roy Gerber, both of whom were divorced and decided to move in together to cut down the cost of their daily living expenses,' the younger Simon has revealed. 'My brother was quite a good cook and housekeeper; he didn't want maid service because that cost too much money, too. He had to give alimony to his wife and pay for his two children – same as Roy. So they were living together and I remember Danny telling me the story of inviting two girls to dinner, because taking them out was a very costly affair. Danny made a roast to be ready at 8.15pm, then discovered Roy hadn't given the girls a firm time to arrive. Danny went mad. His roast was to be ready at 8.15pm, not 8pm or 8.30pm or 9pm. "If they're not here by 8.15, my roast is going to be dried up!" This domestic squabble was not only hilarious, it was also indicative of the problems they had with their wives. Not only was Danny cooking the roast, he was very particular about how the money should be spent, how their lives should be led. Roy was much more lackadaisical, irresponsible, if you will.'

In *The Odd Couple* Simon's brother Danny is

transformed into Felix Unger, a prissy, hypochondriac television executive who beats as he sweeps as he cleans all over the apartment he shares with Oscar Madison following the break up of his marriage. Divorced Oscar is a slovenly, messy sportswriter who stalks the apartment with scant regard for time, cleanliness or personal appearance. When the two are forced to exist in close proximity their opposing personalities are quickly on a collision course. Initially Felix has been suicidal after leaving his wife but soon adjusts to his life as a bachelor, compulsively cleaning, expertly cooking and getting on Oscar's nerves. Oscar finds him so finnicky that he complains, 'he wears a seat belt in a drive-in movie'. Felix leaves notes around the house, 'it took me three hours to figure out that F.U. was Felix Ungar', shrieks Oscar. Eventually Oscar breaks down, driven mad 'cooped up here with Mary Poppins twenty-four hours a day.' He wants them to have some fun, 'and getting a clear picture on Channel Two is not my idea of whoopee.' When Oscar throws a carefully prepared meal over the kitchen wall Felix counters, 'I'm a neurotic nut but you're crazy.' The battle-lines are drawn and the two best friends just can't live under the same roof. Felix moves out but promises to drop around on Friday for the regular weekly poker game.

Packed with laughter lines *The Odd Couple* has a classic clash of opposites that results in both people becoming more understanding. Lunging around stage, Matthau attacked the role of Oscar with expertise and the relish of a man who's time has finally come. Oscar was the major role that had for so long proved elusive in Matthau's career – a fat, juicy lead character in a top script. There were even many elements in that script with which Matthau could associate: he had been a sports coach, enjoyed an interest in writing and could slouch his way through an easygoing lifestyle with the best of them. However, Matthau was quick to dispell any comparisons that went too far: 'In real life I'm much neater than that character. I always notice if there isn't a coaster under a glass – particularly if it's on my table.'

On stage Matthau had an excellent sparring partner in Art Carney, one of the best second bananas in the business who had played the foil to the likes of Jackie Gleason, Edgar Bergen and Fred Allen. Carney's Felix caught the tense, jittery perfectionism of a man whose blood pressure count rises with every minute he spends in contact with Oscar. As the two men fight and jostle they display all the characteristics that must have sunk their respective marriages.

Decked out in a twelve-cents pair of purple dungarees purchased in Chinatown Matthau turned his nightly sparring bout with Carney's fusspot into one of the season's biggest Broadway hits. The two found they could just roar through the invective and insult of the show; one evening Matthau opened his beer can and unexpectedly sprayed the stage with froth; it soon became another part of the show. During the course of the run Matthau lost fifteen pounds in weight and had the time of his life. At one point he asked to swop roles with Carney, 'because it would be more of a challenge', but no one wanted to tamper with a success. He didn't get his way but it gives an indication of his dedication to his craft and versatility that he would ask in the first place. When he felt one of Felix's lines was in bad taste he proved quite devious in his desire to have his way, writing a pseudonymous letter of complaint to Simon while the show was on the road. The offending line was eventually removed.

Matthau was laughing all the way to the top of his profession with *The Odd Couple*, the play that ensured his final elevation to stage stardom, a success crowned by his receipt of the Tony Award as Broadway's Best. 'Suddenly I was laughter boy of the year', Matthau commented. The years of lousy movies and entrenchment in the ranks of the 'also starring' category of performers had ended in middle-age; suddenly, unexpectedly and entirely deservedly. As if to confirm this, *Time* magazine wrote: 'Matthau, 44, is now starring in Broadway's new smash comedy, *The Odd Couple* and he is so bellyachingly funny as the loutish sportswriter that no one will ever forget him again.' No one has.

Chapter Five

Between 1962 and 1965 Matthau had stolen scenes from every major film star with whom he had appeared. It had almost become a Hollywood maxim never to co-star with children, animals and Walter Matthau. On stage the triumph of *The Odd Couple* had consolidated his achievements and now it only required the right script to do the same for him on screen. Suddenly, in middle-age, somebody up there liked him, and that somebody was Billy Wilder.

Austrian-born Wilder had been a sportswriter and one time dance-hall gigolo before heading for America to escape the increasingly ugly political scene in thirties' Europe. In America he quickly established himself as one of the top screenwriters in Hollywood, collaborating with Charles Brackett to produce such memorable fare as *Bluebeard's Eighth Wife* (1938), *Midnight* (1939) and *Ninotchka* (1939). Eventually, with *The Major and the Minor* in 1942, he graduated to directing in America and has been responsible for several of the all-time classics on everyone's list of top films: *Double Indemnity* (1944), *The Lost Weekend* (1945), *Sunset Boulevard* (1950), *Ace in the Hole* (1951), *Stalag 17* (1953) and *Witness for the Prosecution* (1957). Starting with *Some Like It Hot* (1959), Wilder had found the ideal actor to interpret his bittersweet romantic comedies of manners and morals: Jack

Lemmon. Lemmon, like Matthau, had made his entry into the world of showbusiness through stage work and a myriad of appearances during the era of live television. His film debut came in the 1954 feature *It Should Happen to You* where he was introduced to the public as 'an actor you're going to like'. Within two years the likeable, hard-working young performer had won an Oscar as Best Supporting Actor in his role as Ensign Pulver in *Mister Roberts* (1955). After playing second lead to the likes of Glenn Ford in *Cowboy* (1957), Robert Mitchum in *Fire Down Below* (1957) and James Stewart in *Bell, Book and Candle* (1958), Lemmon achieved full comic stardom in *Some Like It Hot* as one half of a duo of musicians forced into female impersonation when they inadvertently witness the St Valentine's Day Massacre and flee Chicago. Billy Wilder has declared, 'happiness is working with Jack Lemmon'. Their partnership had flourished in *The Apartment* (1960) and *Irma La Douce* (1963). Wilder, who had collected six Oscars for his work, was about to team with Lemmon again on a new film, *The Fortune Cookie*, and there was a part in the production for Matthau. It wasn't just *a* part, but *the* part – unscrupulous, shyster lawyer Willie Gingrich, immortalised in the film's British release title, *Meet Whiplash Willie*.

Lemmon had admired Matthau's previous work, although the two did not know each other. Wilder too had kept an eye on Matthau's career for many years. In 1955 he directed *The Seven Year Itch*, adapting the stage success with its original author George Axelrod, then responsible for Matthau's Broadway hit *Will Success Spoil Rock Hunter?* Matthau was the first choice for the lead role in the movie; the ordinary male, free of the family for the summer, and tempted to exercise his seven year itch by the extraordinary female upstairs – Marilyn Monroe.

With Jayne Mansfield, his Broadway co-star in
Will Success Spoil Rock Hunter?
(1955)

A Face in the Crowd (1957) with Patricia Neal

Onionhead (1958) with Andy Griffith

The Fortune Cookie (1966),
winning an Oscar with a little help from his friends, Billy Wilder and Jack Lemmon

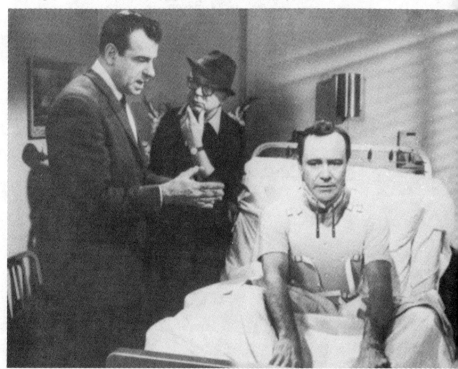

The Odd Couple (1968), recreating his stage success as super slob Oscar

The Odd Couple (1968)
with Jack Lemmon

The great screen lover in
George Axelrod's
*The Secret Life
of an American Wife*
(1968)

Hello Dolly (1969)
with Barbra Streisand

Cactus Flower (1969) with Ingrid Bergman

Plaza Suite (1971) with Lee Grant

A New Leaf (1971)
with the film's writer-director,
Elaine May

However, the then head of Twentieth Century-Fox, Darryl Zanuck, had felt that the role should not be filled by an unknown and insisted on an actor with film experience, finally choosing Tom Ewell who had appeared in *Adam's Rib* (1949) and many other films.

Wilder's 1964 film *Kiss Me Stupid*, starring Dean Martin, had received the most scathing reviews imaginable, vilified as tasteless and crude, which ensured its commercial failure. For *The Fortune Cookie* Wilder had promised Lemmon: 'It's about greed, love, compassion, human understanding but not about sex.' Wilder's inspiration for the film had come while watching a football match on television. As Lemmon would later recall: 'Billy saw a huge fullback make an end sweep, gallop out of bounds and fall right on top of a spectator. He saw this thing and said to himself, "That's a movie and the guy underneath is Lemmon!" Wilder then began fashioning the original idea into a full-length screenplay with his frequent writing partner I.A.L. Diamond. Matthau was approached to play a role in the film and committed himself to the production without reading a script, happy to be working with people of the calibre of Lemmon and Wilder.

When the final script arrived in Matthau's hands he realised that he had the star part, with Lemmon virtually playing a straight role as the fall guy. Lemmon would also be spending almost the entire film in a brace or confined to a wheelchair. Stunned, Matthau contacted Lemmon and asked, 'Why are you doing this when you are the star? It's obvious that I have the far better part.'

Lemmon simply replied, 'Don't you think that it's about time?' Lemmon was well aware that comic stardom for Matthau was long overdue and explained, 'I had tremendous respect for him. He had great talent and we all knew it. It was a case of just not getting the right part or he would have been a star long before he was. I knew his was the part, but I didn't give a damn. I felt my function in that piece was to be the maypole and let the other actors run around me. Anyway, I'll play straight man to him anytime.'

Lemmon's selflessness, in an industry hardly renowned for the abundance of such a quality, was the beginning of a beautiful friendship between the two performers that has endured almost twenty years and five joint film assignments. There is a strong friendship too between the actors' wives, and Carol Matthau has commented, 'Jack is the most generous actor in the world. One thinks of actors as being so narcissistic, they are frightened and therefore selfish and all those things. But not Jack; he just isn't.' Lemmon observed, 'Walter and I hit it off right away. We both love football so that made making the picture more enjoyable. Since then, you might say, we have been almost inseparable.'

When filming began Matthau had to quickly adapt to Wilder's way of direction. Meticulous in his pre-production, Wilder has a fairly set image of how a scene should be performed and, while allowing an actor to rehearse as long as he likes and make any suggestions, the script is, by and large, sacred. 'He has a Germanic habit of wanting every scene done the same way, take after take. I cured him of that. Didn't listen to a word he said. And on the third day he told me to do something I didn't agree with and I said to him, "You speak kind of funny Billy – are you from out of town?" I think he got the message,' Matthau has said.

Lemmon, Wilder and Matthau were enjoying working on *The Fortune Cookie* when, well into the film's production, Matthau was felled by a major heart attack. 'Suddenly my heart started to tock more than tick. And my doc shook his head like they do in a B-film deathbed scene', Matthau joked. The heart attack could have severely jeopardised Matthau's participation in *The Fortune Cookie*. When Billy Wilder filmed *Kiss Me Stupid* he was thrilled with the material starring Peter Sellers, before the British star suffered a massive coronary. For financial reasons alone the decision had to be taken to replace him and, once Ray Walston was signed as a replacement, production began again. The same situation could have transpired on *The Fortune Cookie*. The costs involved in suspending shooting, the growing interest charges on the investment in the production and the problem of retaining the initial enthusiasm among the cast and crew must have pressed strongly on the minds of those debating whether or not to halt production or replace Matthau.

That they chose to wait for Matthau to recover has largely been credited to his wife Carol, giving the performance of her life. 'I lied to everyone. At first I told them it was indigestion, that we were taking him to hospital for tests. Then I said it wasn't a serious heart attack and that all he needed was a little rest. I was stalling and trying to find something each day that was good to tell Walter. I would talk to Jack every evening; talk in circles, delaying. I didn't know then what it meant to hold up film productions – the cost and such or I might not have done what I did. One evening I was talking with Jack and not telling him the truth, and just before I hung up he said, "Carol, there's something I want you to know. You never have to level with me."

'That was such a beautiful thing to do at such a terrible time. It let me off the hook; it was the most graceful, generous gesture.'

Seven weeks after his heart attack Matthau returned to work on *The Fortune Cookie*. The discrepancy between his pre-and post-attack appearance was glaring. Just before filming had been suspended Matthau had filmed the scene in which he rushes upstairs to present Lemmon's character with the cheque in settlement of his fraudulent insurance claim. When Matthau returned the scene was completed with him entering the room to present the cheque to Lemmon. 'You see me going upstairs weighing a hundred and ninety-eight pounds. I walk in and I'm a hundred and sixty pounds.' Such continuity problems aside, the filming was completed without further interruption.

In *The Fortune Cookie*, Lemmon plays Harry Hinkle, a CBS sports cameraman, who is covering the Cleveland Browns-Minnesota Vikings game one icy Sunday afternoon. During the game Hinkle is involved in an accident when a two-hundred-and-twenty-pound halfback, Luther 'Boom, Boom' Jackson (Ron Rich) comes crashing his way, leaving poor Harry out cold. In the Wilder-Diamond screenplay there is the following observation: 'His name is Harry Hinkle, and he will be thirty-six next September. That makes him a Virgo – and if he had read his horoscope, he would've stayed in bed today.'

Hinkle comes round in hospital, suffering from mild concussion. At least that's what he thinks he's suffering from until the arrival of his brother-in-law, the opportunity-grabbing Willie Gingrich (Matthau). The dollar signs light up in Willie's eyes as he schemes to exploit the situation for maximum gain. If Harry will pretend to be in pain, Willie plans an assault on the assets of the team, the stadium and the television company to the value of one million dollars. Old X-rays of Harry's previous spinal injury will satisfy the experts and Willie has a watertight case. 'They've got so much money they don't know what to do with it. They've run out of storage space. They have to microfilm it,' he gleefully asserts.

Harry is basically a decent guy who would never dream of involving himself in a fraudulent insurance claim, but Willie appeals to the chink in his armour of decency – the torch he still carries for his estranged wife Sandy (Judi West). Willie argues that the money will allow the couple a second chance and Sandy is equally willing to exploit the hapless Harry.

Confined to a wheelchair Harry observes all humanity around him – the unbridled greed of Willie, the hypocrisy of Sandy and the conscience-stricken 'Boom, Boom', convinced that he has permanently crippled Harry. He receives the settlement cheque but is sickened by the whole farrago. He gets some sound advice from the message inside a fortune cookie: 'You can fool all of the people some of the time, and some of the people all of the time – but you can't fool all of the people all of the time.' Harry frees himself from the brace, tumbling and somersaulting around his apartment to expose the fraud to a dogged private-eye who has been watching the building for some time. Free once again he seeks out 'Boom, Boom' to make amends.

Clever, witty and beautifully acted, *The Fortune Cookie* was warmly welcomed for putting Wilder back in a familiar vein of cynical, moralistic black comedy. After all, to Wilder, a cynic is merely, 'a romantic with twenty-twenty vision'. Matthau's sly, conniving shyster lawyer does tend to dominate the film, throwing the moral argument off balance. His corrupt wheeler-dealing is done with such skill and adroitness that he is viewed with admiring awe while it is Lemmon's decent, common man who should be gaining maximum sympathy. However, as first-rate Wilder entertainment it was a triumph.

Lemmon and Matthau received excellent reviews on both sides of the Atlantic and a new star-teaming was born with an abundance of that undefinable commodity – chemistry. In America Judith Crist wrote, in the *World Journal Tribune*, 'The old Billy Wilder is back with *The Fortune Cookie* and a case of grand and glorious larceny committed by Walter Matthau, who walks away with everything in sight and sound', whilst *Time* magazine observed: 'Actor Matthau is leering, sneering, sniggering, swaggering, popping his optics, slopping his chops and generally behaving like the Nero of the Nuisance Claims Division.' In Britain, Alexander Walker of the *Evening Standard* was at his most eloquent when he stated: 'Whiplash Willie, as incarnated by Matthau's dyspeptic frog's countenance, has a crocodile's eye for the main chance, the patience of a leech and a bite like a bear trap when an insurance company crosses his tracks.

'He is droopy but Snoopy, limp but alert – he makes the usual ambulance-chasing lawyers look as if their brains are in their feet. Whiplash lets nothing come between him and the insurance men's money, except the settlement cheque.'

In 1967, when his Hollywood colleagues came around to considering the best performances of the previous year, Matthau was nominated for the Academy Award as Best Supporting Actor of 1966. The nomination could equally well have come in the Best Actor category, but who was to carp at the Academy's distinction. His fellow nominees were the Japanese-American actor Mako for *The Sand Pebbles*, James Mason (who had never previously won the Oscar) for *Georgy Girl*, George Segal for *Who's Afraid of Virginia Woolf?* and Robert Shaw for *A Man for All Seasons*. The latter two nominations came from a couple of films that dominated the awards that year.

The award ceremony was set for 10 April 1967 at the Civic Auditorium in Santa Monica. The event almost missed being televised because of a threatened strike by the American Federation of Television and Radio Artists. However, the dispute with the network was resolved two hours before the ceremony began and the estimated viewing public of sixty-five million could rest assured that they would miss none of the drama inherent in one of television's hardy perennials. Matthau almost didn't make the ceremony himself. The previous Sunday he had fallen from his bicycle while riding along the Pacific Coast Highway and arrived on the uncharacteristically showery April day with his right arm in a plaster cast.

The 1967 event, with Bob Hope as master of ceremonies, had a galaxy of stars from Hollywood's Golden Age acting as presenters – Fred Astaire and Ginger Rogers tripped the light fantastic for old times' sake and other presenters included Rosalind Russell, Bette Davis, Irene Dunne, Olivia De Havilland, James Stewart, Fred MacMurray and Robert Mitchum. Patricia Neal, returning to public view after her valiant struggle to overcome the effects of a crippling series of strokes, received a standing ovation from her colleagues in the industry.

There is an Academy Awards tradition whereby the Best Supporting Actor award is presented by the previous year's winner in the Best Supporting Actress category. Thus it fell to Shelley Winters to announce the winner for 1966. And the winner was Walter Matthau for *The Fortune Cookie*. The other Oscar winners in the acting categories, Elizabeth Taylor, Paul Scofield and Sandy Dennis, were not present to accept their awards but Matthau was and he ambled up to the stage, a winner popular with the assembled celebrities. One report of the ceremony said, 'his acceptance speech was one of the evening's few with a bit of humour. He said he had been

71

given a great deal of money for playing a juicy part with beautiful people and that getting an Oscar, in addition, was "well, a bit too much".'

Matthau, referring to his recent heart attack, wryly observed: 'They wanted to give me something for all my long years of achievement before I died.'

Chapter Six

Time magazine once said that Matthau was 'about as likely a candidate for superstardom as the neighbourhood delicatessen man', yet in the late sixties that was exactly the position in which he found himself: a superstar, the oldest overnight success in the history of show-business. In middle-age he had become a bankable movie star with a group of friends and colleagues lining up to sing his praises. After filming *The Fortune Cookie* Billy Wilder commented: 'As far as I'm concerned Walter can play anything from Rhett Butler to Scarlett O'Hara. They call him a second W.C. Fields but he's much more than that. He's like a decathlon champion who could be a world champion in each of the ten events. The time has come when Matthau can play the lead, carry the picture. He has an appeal to women, and audiences identify with him. He's everybody's brother-in-law.'

Everybody's brother-in-law was also fast becoming one of Jack Lemmon's favourite co-stars and one of his greatest friends off screen. Lemmon said of him: 'He has what I consider the greatest single face in the world as an actor. It is the map of every human emotion.'

Inundated with requests for interviews and stories, Matthau himself was at pains to probe his sudden rise to stardom. In several press articles he assessed the various factors: 'Fashions in leading men have changed. It's as simple as that. Anybody with a big nose, little lips and beady eyes looks like me. It's been said I remind people of their favourite uncle. Fifteen or twenty years ago they wanted handsome, smooth, poetic types – whether they could act or not. Sometimes they could – sometimes they were just sticks of wood. But decorative sticks. Now they're looking for actors. That's partly why there's such a wave of Britishers around the screen these days, most of them – Finney, Burton, Caine – not at all matinée idol types. Simply good actors. And we've got 'em too, look at James Coburn and George Segal.'

As to why it had taken him so long to reach the top he believed: 'I have to assume that I've been giving the best performances in the world over the past twenty years or so but in a whole series of resounding flops. That may sound like a pretty unlucky run but, on the other hand, I didn't always get the breaks. Listen, if you're no good when the right moment comes you never were and you never will be. I like to think I wasn't just a bum until I got lucky – in fact, I'm trying to avoid using the word talent – but I don't underestimate the importance of doing the right thing at the right time.' Much later he would add: 'It was all so unexpected. I'd been around for so long I was quite sure that stardom had passed me by. Audiences became interested in the anti-hero. They didn't want their heroes too beautiful any more so the pretty guys were relegated to the character parts. I think that was an excellent result, that shift of power. Thank God, I was on the winning side. It would have been murder to have been handsome and beautiful – and neglected.'

Neglected he certainly wasn't. Continuing to live in New York and now following a regime of long daily walks and exercise for his heart condition he was faced with some important decisions over his future. The heart

74

attack had been a warning to slow down and, much as he enjoyed the demands placed on a performer by stage work, he considered filming less exhausting and certainly better paid. Now he could even afford to gamble in the style to which he had become accustomed, although with the financial rewards that stardom entailed he no longer had cause for concern in that department.

After much persuasion he accepted a film to be directed by Gene Kelly, entitled *A Guide for the Married Man*. With the close of the great era of the original Hollywood musical Kelly had chosen to channel his talents into other areas, straight acting and direction. In the latter capacity Kelly had filmed the 1958 Doris Day comedy *The Tunnel of Love* and *Gigot* a 1962 vehicle for Jackie Gleason. Although Matthau was less than enamoured of the script he undertook the lead role of Paul Manning.

Manning is a happily married man, an ordinary fellow with a loving, attentive and faithful wife Ruth (Inger Stevens). However, an unvarying diet of fidelity and affection makes him wonder what it might be like to stray from the fold just once. On hand to offer him expert advice is his neighbour Ed Stander (Robert Morse), a self-confessed master of undetected extra-marital activities. Ed firmly believes that a man makes a better husband if he remains interested in other women, but counsels: 'Never have an affair with someone who doesn't have as much to lose as you do.'

Ed then proceeds to illustrate his list of dos and don'ts in everyday adultery, providing Paul with the married man's guide. Paul is persuaded that his life is missing an exciting element of danger and embarks on his first affair. He agrees to meet divorcée Jocelyn Montgomery (Elaine Devoy) in an isolated hotel but decides to chicken out at the last moment and is alarmingly discouraged when, in the same hotel, Ed is discovered at play by Mrs Stander and a group of witnesses. Paul flees back to the safety of his wife and the soundtrack intones a chorus of 'There's No Place Like Home'.

At heart, *A Guide for the Married Man* is basically a string of sketches and one-liners on the theme of infidelity performed by a starry pack of jokers that included Lucille Ball, Jack Benny, Art Carney, Jayne Mansfield, Phil Silvers and Terry-Thomas. Matthau's ordinary Joe is the glue and string which keeps the whole package together. He's really not the wandering, errant-husband but just a poor fall-guy persuaded that he's missing out on something. One of the film's jokes is delivered in the line, 'This is the best steak money can buy. But every now and then I feel like fish.' The moral of the film is that you're better staying with the steak.

At the time Kelly was challenged as to the dubious morality of a film intent on giving a guide to how to cheat on your wife. He defended the film, saying, 'Sure *A Guide for the Married Man* shows every trick in the book on how to deceive your wife and get away with it. But what happens? Walter Matthau, who plays the married man with the twelve year itch, never does get to stray. He runs like a homing pigeon back to his wife, whom he loves all the time anyway. And who wouldn't, with Inger Stevens to come home to. She's a pretty lovable girl.'

A Guide for the Married Man was hardly a great comic film but it was a crowd pleaser and, in America, wound up at the number eighteen position in the list of top box-office films in 1967, with five million dollars to its credit. The Matthau name was on another success, no bad thing for an advancing film career and, waiting in the wings, was the more challenging prospect of filming *The Odd Couple*.

There are no guaranteed rules when it comes to putting stage successes on film. All kinds of tampering and re-jigging can occur during the transformation and the odds on whether the stage actors remain in their original roles are probably none too favourable. The film of *Will Success Spoil Rock Hunter?* which Matthau had appeared in on stage, starred Jayne Mansfield and Tony Randall while *A Shot in the Dark* ended up as the backbone for a Peter Sellers' Inspector Clouseau farce. Fortunately *The Odd Couple* survived the transition relatively unscathed with Neil Simon adapting his own play. Now an established film star, it would have been unthinkable for Matthau not to have recreated his role of super-slob Oscar but Art Carney wasn't allowed to reprise his part of the fussy Felix. Instead he was passed over in favour of Jack Lemmon, and *The Fortune Cookie* team was reunited. Matthau didn't object because the two actors were now so close: 'I wouldn't say we're like brothers but we're very chummy cousins. We're too different to be brothers, but we have the best chemistry this side of Tracy and Hepburn! I love working with him.'

Paramount had previously filmed Neil Simon's *Barefoot in the Park* with Jane Fonda and Robert Redford under the direction of Gene Saks, more accustomed to working on Broadway. More than pleased with the results, Paramount wanted Saks to do a similar job on *The Odd Couple*. Lemmon, reputedly receiving one and a half million dollars for his participation, had the contractual right of directorial approval and was placed in a considerable dilemma as he knew that Billy Wilder had expressed a keen interest in making *The Odd Couple*. Lemmon eventually chose not to disapprove of Saks, as he had no legitimate reason for complaint and Paramount was happy to employ the less expensive talent of the Broadway director. Columnists sought to blow the incident into a full-scale rift between Lemmon and Wilder but to little avail. Lemmon simply stated, 'It would have been very interesting to see what Billy would have done with the material. His concept would have been completely different.'

Under Saks the production sailed smoothly ahead and finished one week ahead of schedule. Originally Paramount had believed that Lemmon would want to play the richer comic part of Oscar, and that Matthau would be content playing Felix. However, the film's producer had the good sense to dispel any such notions, telling Matthau that he was born to play Oscar and that was exactly what he was going to do. Filming went so well that Lemmon could genuinely report,' 'I've never enjoyed working with an actor more than Walter Matthau in *The Odd Couple*. Many actors work at you and it can get very lonely out there with someone acting at you. But Walter's interested in making the scene work. I'll give you an example. In a scene in *The Odd Couple* I said, "I'm not so bad, you know. It could be worse." And he was supposed to say, "How?" So in rehearsal I said it and then, for the hell of it, I turned and walked out of the room, slammed the door and left him standing there with the line. He came right after me. He pushed open the door, stuck his head through – just his head – and said, "How?" It was a joy. Walter is a helluvan actor, the best I've ever worked with.'

The Odd Couple was a comic triumph despite some rather lack-lustre direction from Saks, who seemed intent on an excessive and unattractive use of close-ups. Simon's saga of the two media men whose combative domestic lifestyle leads to a better understanding of their individual prejudices and behavioural quirks, transfers well to the screen with all the laugh lines intact. Lemmon plays the finnicky, pernickety Felix virtually straight, extracting pathos from the part and underscoring the melancholy inherent in a man who is 'Nothing without my wife and kids'. Matthau is superb, swooping and lunging in a malevolent predatory fashion on every line and situation that comes his way. It is a virtuoso display of timing and characterisation by an acknowledged master who can sense the comic potential in a line with the unerring instinct of a trained pig in search of truffles. *The Odd Couple* received virtually unanimous critical acclaim, typical of which was Judith Crist in *New York* Magazine, who wrote: 'A funny thing happened at Radio City Music Hall this week and more I can't wish but it should happen to you. *The Odd Couple*, one of the very best comedies to have emanated from Broadway in recent years, arrived on screen not only intact but actually enhanced by the transition.' *Time* magazine, always a Matthau supporter, agreed, stating, 'The film owes it's comic force to the two stars – one visible, the other unseen. Walter Matthau, with his loping, sloping style, mangled grin and laugh-perfect timing, may well be America's finest comic actor. And playwright Neil Simon occasionally takes off his clown's masks to show the human beneath.' The film was also very much to public taste, grossing eighteen and a half million dollars during its 1968 release in America, a figure surpassed by only four other films that year – *The Graduate, Guess Who's Coming to Dinner?*, a reissue of *Gone With the Wind* and *Valley of the Dolls*.

Two smash hits were followed in quick succession by two flops: *Candy* and *The Secret Life of an American Wife*, the latter unjustly cold-shouldered by the public. Assessing the rewards conferred by stardom Matthau has said, 'The biggest kick I get is being bankable. That means if a producer takes a dirty poem down to the bank and says that you've read it and you're willing to play the lead the guy gives him the money to turn it into a movie. This certainly seems to be pretty much the way *Candy* came to be made.

The major Hollywood studios had steered clear of any attempts to film the 'unfilmable' book by Terry Southern and Mason Hoffenburg which detailed the adventures of an Alice in sexual wonderland. In 1967 actor-director Christian Marquand managed to engage the interest of his good friend Marlon Brando in acting in *Candy* and an independent production was set up. Marquand explained: 'In the beginning it was Marlon Brando who read the book and thought it would make a delightful spoof. We talked about it and he thought Richard Burton might be interested in one of the major roles, that of McPhisto, the touring Welsh poet.

'Richard roared when we discussed it, and from there, it was a matter of talking with the production companies, which isn't difficult when you have two of the world's great actors already agreed.' The then Mrs Burton, Elizabeth Taylor, politely declined the role of Aunt Livia but Marquand managed to assemble the four million dollar production funds on the lure of the Brando-Burton names.

Buck Henry, a writer for the 'Get Smart' television series and author of *The Graduate*, was designated scriptwriter and Marquand set out to find his Candy. This task was almost on a par with the famed search for Scarlett O'Hara, with over two thousand applicants screened during the shortlisting process, including Susan George. The ultimate choice was the Swedish starlet, Ewa Aulin, a beauty queen renowned as Miss Teen International of 1966.

Production began in November 1967 with filming scheduled in Rome, New York and San Francisco. Buck

Henry declared that his script had a treatment as 'Rough and irreverent as that of the novel, faithful in spirit rather than detail. I am tailoring the roles to suit the collection of superstars who are acting cameo parts.' Marquand had assembled an assorted bag of celebrities, beautiful people and even the odd actor to play the men in Candy's life. Among the guilty parties were Burton, Ringo Starr as a Mexican gardener, Charles Aznavour as a hunchback, Brando as an Indian guru, James Coburn as a surgeon and Matthau as General Smight, all intent on leading Candy away from the path of righteousness. Interestingly there were two former screen stars who had preferred to remain in retirement rather than answer Marquand's call to work: Shirley Temple and Ronald Reagan, then Governor of California. Reagan had been offered his choice from two roles, one half of Siamese twins or a deranged meat inspector!

Matthau's General Smight is one true blue patriot, paranoid over the lesser mortals attempting to undermine the US of A – commie sympathisers, subscribers to the *New York Times*, patrons of foreign films and fanciers of caviar. Prepared at all times to face the threat from these sources Smight and his men make their permanent quarters in an aeroplane ready for instant action. When Candy appears Smight hasn't left the aeroplane for six years and is obviously more than happy to lay eyes on the attractive nymphet.

Asked how he intended to play his Dr Strangelove-style character, Matthau replied, 'I'm going to play against it. A man on the right is usually many times expressionless and inflectionless. I plan to play inflectionless.' In Rome he claims to have spent his time chasing cockroaches around his deluxe hotel suite. As to his reasons for accepting the role, one can only guess. The 'dirty poem' factor probably came into it; or he may have been attracted by the off-beat humour of the role.

When *Candy* was released at Christmas time in 1968 the critical knives were out and the film, by and large, was scathingly treated. The *New York Times'* reviewer, Renata Adler believed, 'the movie, directed by Christian Marquand, manages to compromise, by its relentless, crawling, bloody lack of talent, almost anyone who had anything to do with it.' In general Matthau was one of the few stars to escape with his reputation intact.

Around this time Matthau was tentatively committed to appearing in the comedy-drama *The Night They Raided Minskys*, and an offer to work with George Axelrod on a film in Hollywood was also in the pipe-line. According to Matthau he had a bitter dispute with his mother who had threatened to kill his wife Carol. 'My wife said she wasn't afraid because she knew mother was too cheap to hire anybody,' he joked. Serious or not, it was considered a judicious moment to put a little space between the warring sides in the family argument. The more Matthau learned of the Axelrod project the more attractive it became. He would be paid a half-million dollars, most of the film took place in bed and he could choose his leading lady. 'It was too beautiful to resist. I gave up *Minskys* and took that picture – and that's how movies are made!'

Since their last professional meeting on *Goodbye Charlie*, George Axelrod had widened his talents by not only writing but also directing *Lord Love a Duck* (1966), a well received black comedy starring Roddy McDowall and Tuesday Weld. Now he had returned his attention to the consideration of the sexual hang-ups of his fellow Americans, with a script known at various stages as *The Connecticut Look*, *The Feminine Mistake* and, finally, *The Secret Life of An American Wife*. With Anne Jackson, a long-time Matthau admirer, set to play the wife, filming began with Axelrod advising the actor, 'Don't try to be peculiar: just accept the fact that you are peculiar and behave as normally as you can.'

Described by Axelrod as 'the other side of the Seven Year Itch', *The Secret Life of An American Wife* begins with Victoria Layton (Anne Jackson) in bed with her husband, delivering a monologue direct to the camera establishing the deadly domestic routine into which her suburban existence has tumbled. Her husband, a PR man, is ignoring her, spending more time bowing and scraping to his clients, her children are away at school and, at thirty-four, she considers 'my life is finished'.

One morning Tom Layton (Patrick O'Neal) leaves to minister to his biggest-paying client, a world-weary movie star (Matthau). Analysing her life, Victoria begins to fantasise a more exciting existence and decides to pass herself off as a hooker and spend the afternoon with the sex symbol. After all, she reckons, 'what a glorious way to make a living, doing something you enjoy and getting paid for it.'

The afternoon of pleasure doesn't unfold as expected. Victoria tends the movie star's ailments with chicken soup and the two unburden themselves of their individual problems. The movie star discusses the difficulty of maintaining an image of a hell-raiser when you're fifty-one, Victoria is concerned with the PTA and the cooling of the passion in her marriage. The couple make love and Victoria returns contentedly to the family roost. Her husband meanwhile has quit his job, punching the movie star on the chin to reassert his independence. The married couple may now be poorer but they are out of the rut.

Axelrod here stresses the common thread in all human experience and fears – worries of ageing, love and passion. A pleasure-seeking hedonistic movie star with a staff of seventy-three and a fictitious image as a swinger shares a lot with a suburban housewife upset by kids that desire only maple syrup and frozen pizza for breakfast. A modish comedy of manners probing the sexual psyche of America, *Secret Life of An American Wife* provided a choice male role in 'the movie star', a part for any actor to sink his teeth into. It's a measure of the fact that Matthau wasn't just any actor that he chose to underplay the role beautifully, lightly under-scoring the humanising elements in the aloof movie star's make-up. In America Axelrod's wordy, sophisticated confection was a flop although he loved his stint in the director's chair. 'The secret is to have more enegy than the rest of the people on the film combined. I never sit down. It cuts about three days off a picture if you're pacing up and down behind the cameraman when he's lighting.'

The American reactions prejudiced the film's marketing in Britain where it was thrown away on the lower half of a double-bill with the Frank Sinatra detective yarn *Lady in Cement*, despite a warm reception at the London Film Festival and from the British press. Axelrod bemoaned the film's fate: 'The businessmen moved in. I saw it coming. One studio boss said he'd made a million dollars out of flour without knowing anything about the stuff and he could do the same in movies. They think making a movie is like making cornflakes.' Axelrod has not directed since.

Chapter Seven

Hello, Dolly! starring Carol Channing opened on Broadway on 16 January 1964 and ran for two thousand, eight hundred and forty-four performances, picking up an impressive nine Tony Awards along the way.

Twentieth Century-Fox, on the crest of the wave with its highly successful film *The Sound of Music*, purchased the screen rights for two and a half million dollars plus a percentage of the gross and with a built-in proviso that no film would be released until the show closed, or before 20 June 1971, whichever came first. Influenced by *The Sound of Music* profits and concluding that the public appetite was now whetted for lavish, big-budget musicals the studio had decided to invest in *Dr Dolittle,Star* and *Hello, Dolly!* It almost caused them to go bankrupt.

The *Hello, Dolly!* show was simply the most recent incarnation of some well tried and tested material. In 1835 there had been a play *A Day Well Spent* by John Oxenford which had been followed in 1842 by a German adaptation. In 1938 Thornton Wilder adapted the play for Broadway, retitled it *The Merchant of Yonkers* and had a flop on his hands. Returning to the subject in 1953 he refashioned it into *The Matchmaker* and had a hit, filmed in 1958 with Shirley Booth and a cast that included Anthony Perkins and Shirley Maclaine. The show that opened on Broadway obviously had a distinguished pedigree and the Fox executives, led by studio head Richard Zanuck, were determined to spare no expense. Screenwriter Ernest Lehman who had written *North By Northwest* and acted as producer on *Who's Afraid of Virginia Woolf?* was assigned to produce what promised to be a mammoth undertaking.

The immediate talking point in Hollywood concerned who was to play Dolly, the warmhearted, middle-aged matchmaker. At various stages of the Broadway run Dolly had provided a late-career hit for Ginger Rogers and Betty Grable. Carol Channing had spent almost four years in the part. However, the value of these ladies at the cinema box-offices was dubious. Grable had not appeared in a film since the mid-fifties, Rogers appeared to have retired after *Harlow* in 1965 and Channing had never been allowed to star in a film. Fox dallied with the idea of playing safe and enlisting the services of Julie Andrews, who must have been offered every major musical of the period. Lehman considered his Oscar-winning Martha from *Virginia Woolf*, Elizabeth Taylor, but his first choice was Channing, forever associated in the public mind with a role she had made her own. However, he was persuaded that the idea of over two hours of the irrepressible Miss Channing oozing from neighbourhood cinemas would be a little overpowering.

Eventually none of the more mature contenders for the role were left in the running. They were out-distanced by Barbra Streisand, a mere twenty-five when filming began. Brooklyn-born Streisand had displayed her talents on stage, television and discs but was still an unknown film commodity at this time. Her first film, *Funny Girl*, which would bring her an Oscar was, as yet, unreleased. None the less Twentieth Century-Fox had sufficient confidence in her ability to engage her at a reported fee of three-quarters of a million dollars and a percentage of the takings.

At heart *Hello, Dolly!* is a straightforward tale of the gentle thaw in the character of a grouchy, mean merchant engineered by a widowed matchmaker, Dolly Levi (Streisand) in the New York of the eighteen-nineties. Tight-fisted Horace Vandergelder (Matthau) has engaged the services of the matchmaker to bring about his marriage to Irene Molloy, a young milliner whom Horace views as a perfect housekeeper, dishwasher, handy woman and companion (in that order). Dolly is also to bring Horace's niece Ermengarde (Joyce Ames) to New York to prevent her marrying Ambrose (Tommy Tune) a penniless artist. Horace leaves for New York to march in the 14th Street Association parade and propose to Irene. His two clerks, Cornelius Hackl (Michael Crawford) and Barnaby Tucker (Danny Locke), who have never been allowed a day's holiday, are left in charge of the business but close the store and head for New York as well.

After a number of complications in New York at the Harmonica Gardens, Horace is outraged to find Ambrose and Ermengarde dancing together (thanks to Dolly), distraught to find Cornelius and Barnaby on the town (thanks to Dolly) and insulted by a few home truths from a fake countess (arranged by Dolly). He storms back to Yonkers in a rage. However, in New York he has seen Dolly in a new light, as a beautiful and popular woman, and realises that he wants to marry her, just as Dolly has planned. He blesses the engagement between Ermengarde and Ambrose, makes Cornelius his partner, promotes Barnaby to head clerk and asks Dolly to be his wife.

Filming *Dolly* became an enterprise akin to a military

operation with Gene Kelly needing all his experience, good humour and tolerance to keep hold of events. The eighteen-ninety period interiors and Manhattan exteriors would be shot at the Twentieth Century-Fox studio in Hollywood, the Yonkers exteriors were to be filmed on locations at Garrison and Cold Springs in New York and a grand finale would take place against the sweeping vista of the Hudson River. Construction of the New York set began on 23 October 1967. In January 1968 the film's choreographer Michael Kidd began working on routines with the chorus players and on 19 February the main stars began rehearsing with Kelly and Kidd.

Dolly became one of the most expensive films ever made and produced enough statistics to fill a book. The New York set cost in excess of two million dollars, involving a complex of sixty buildings reproducing Fifth Avenue, Broadway and the Bowery. Running through the area was a six-hundred-foot construction of the Sixth Avenue elevated railway with a working steam engine and three cars. Involved in all this construction were ten tons of nails, three hundred and thirty thousand square feet of plywood, two hundred and twenty tons of steel and more than fifty thousand plastic leaves and blossoms which were hand-tied to plaster trees. On top of this was the opulent Harmonica Gardens set where extras were asked to simulate a happy evening out with real food and drink: one extra claimed to have gained eight pounds in ten days. Most expensive of all was the street parade which cost about $200,000 a day on top of the normal production costs. It was estimated that more than twenty-two thousand extras worked on the film and a group of them took the unprecedented step of paying for an advert in a film trade paper thanking Kelly, Lehman and Richard Zanuck for providing employment in an otherwise lean year.

However, at the core of the production were two personalities who just could not work together – Matthau and Streisand. Streisand had always believed herself miscast in the part but was determined to prove all the doubters wrong, worrying and fretting over every shot and note, like the perfectionist she undoubtedly is. Her devout dedication jarred with the more relaxed approach to filming that Matthau took and he began to find working with her extremely difficult. To be fair to both, Streisand was under tremendous pressure to turn an expensive film into a box-office success; she was too young for the part, she was relatively inexperienced and vulnerable to the sniping of the critics who found her behaviour made good copy: Matthau, too, must have worried about the tremendous costs of filming, about finding a rapport with someone he found unsympathetic, and tolerating the demands of a performer in her twenties who had made only one previous film. Both had worries and problems but, unable to support each other, they retired to their respective corners and came out fighting. She called him Old Sewermouth, he retaliated with a description of her as Miss Ptomaine.

The amiable Gene Kelly attempted to keep the peace but when filming shifted to the hot, muggy New York locations where temperatures were reaching more than ninety-five degrees and both stars were dressed in period costume, tempers became frayed. The assassination of Bobby Kennedy had cast a gloom over the production and set everyone on edge. Matthau exploded, telling Streisand to stop interfering and trying to run the whole show. Streisand gave as good as she got, pointing out that she was the star of the show and that he should stop behaving as if the film were called 'Hello, Walter'.

Later, Kelly commented, 'It wasn't until we were well

into the picture that I realised Barbra was uncomfortable. I asked her why and she admitted she was scared of the part, feeling, like most everybody else, that she was too young for Dolly. She said she thought Elizabeth Taylor would have been a better choice. I had to reassure her and explain that she had to find ways to make up for this change in concept, to look for other things in the part, and she did. But she was very insecure. I had some trepidation about working with her because she had a reputation for being difficult but I didn't find her so. I asked William Wyler and Vincente Minnelli if they had had any problems with her and they said they hadn't. I'd been told she had had some people fired but I couldn't find any proof of that either. She certainly is direct in her manner and her opinions but I prefer that.'

On set Streisand tried to keep cool with the aid of a small electric fan and tended to the needs of her eighteen-month-old son Jason. She remarked, 'Doing this is just like having a baby, very uncomfortable at the time – but you reckon you'll be proud of your efforts later.' She certainly drove herself hard in the exacting task at hand, consuming mountains of food for the filming of the restaurant scene where she devours turkey, dumplings and beetroot whilst rejecting a marriage proposal that Horace is unaware that he has made. She also endured the ninety-eight degree heat to perfect the 'Before the Parade Passes By' scene and declared to reporters that the stage show was, 'A piece of fluff. But when everybody was against me as Dolly I took up the challenge.'

From Matthau's viewpoint she was too grimly determined to make it all work, pushing too hard, trying too much and sometimes forgetting the needs of her fellow performers. In a typical comment he noted, 'I had no disagreements with Barbra Streisand I was merely exasperated at her tendency to be a complete megalomaniac.' In a less humorous mood he was prone to describe the experience as an 'absolute nightmare'.

Despite the dissension filming was completed within ninety days, remarkably just one day over schedule, which was in part due to the infectious enthusiasm and verve displayed by Kelly in his director's role. He even found the time to take charge of the masses of extras in a style likened by Fox's publicity to 'a college cheer leader with humour'. Scrutinising the correct period costumes and accoutrements Kelly asked the assembled mass what the time was. When a few responded he declared, 'Now I've got you! Put those wristwatches away! This camera sees everything.' Kelly also supervised the removal of any fashionable beads and necklaces. 'If you will observe the ladies around you, you will see that ladies had hips in those days – but hippies had we not,' he said. Kelly's drive provided a welcome injection of good humour to a mammoth, time-consuming production where maintaining the interest and energy of all involved was crucial.

The film was ready for public view by February 1969 but, unfortunately for Fox, David Merrick's Broadway production was still running which meant that they were contractually bound not to release the film until 1971. *Hello, Dolly!* had cost Fox a fortune, ultimately some figure between twenty and twenty-five million dollars, and they needed to recoup their investment as quickly as possible. Interest charges would have been crippling and it made greater sense to work out a second settlement with David Merrick than to keep running to the bank. It is believed that Fox paid Merrick a further sum (between one and two million dollars) to allow the film to open in 1969 as well as guaranteeing to reimburse him if the show's gross fell below $60,000 a week during an agreed period. In the ultimate reckoning Merrick made far more from Fox than Fox are ever likely to make from *Hello, Dolly!*

Hello, Dolly! was all set to be released as a blockbusting roadshow with inflated ticket prices, an intermission and all the paraphernalia of a major event. However, the bubble for that particular kind of entertainment had burst with a vengeance when films like *Dr Dolittle* and *Star* had proved severe box-office disappointments. In the gap between *Dolly* opening on Broadway and appearing on film there had been a shift in movie tastes with the removal of some censorship barriers and the opening up of the youth market. The audience that went to *The Sound of Music* in 1965 was less likely to materialise four years later when *Easy Rider* and *Midnight Cowboy* were the big box-office attractions. Whilst there was still an audience for the solid virtues of professionalism and entertainment as embodied in hits like *True Grit* and *Airport*, *Hello, Dolly!* was an old-fashioned film that found the going hard in the circumstances of its 1969 release. With a price tag in excess of twenty million dollars to live up to it would have had to be a huge success just to break even. In any event, *Hello, Dolly!* returned a highly creditable fifteen million dollars in domestic rentals to the much depleted Fox coffers. This would have been a good figure for almost any other film, but it still left this one heavily in the red.

Hello, Dolly! is a tuneful and entertaining musical, sumptuously produced, grandly directed and as good as virtually any screen incarnation of a Broadway show. Despite, or maybe even because of, their on-set bickering Matthau and Streisand do strike sparks off each other – he, well cast, in a Scrooge-like characterisation as the Yonkers hay-seed merchant; and she spiritedly defying her less than ideal casting as the calculating matchmaker. The film has many pleasures including the set piece rendition of the title number with Louis Armstrong and the unexpected bonus of Matthau singing. One British reviewer summed up Matthau's musical ability by saying: 'he doesn't so much sing as moo gently'. The film generally received mixed notices in the States, although it was warmly welcomed by most critics in Britain. In America it was open season on Streisand; *Time* magazine for instance came out against her performance, 'her mannerisms (are) so arch and calculated that one half expects to find a key implanted in her back.'

Kelly certainly didn't regret his involvement with *Hello, Dolly!*, his best film as a director. 'It's not the kind of film I would make as a first choice but what else is there? To make an original musical today you first have to find someone to put up a million dollars, just to develop the idea and that's too much of a risk. What happens now is that studios buy stage shows after they are already dated and then spend a lot of money turning them into dated movies. The musical is the victim of changing times. To make good musicals you need a team of performers, musicians, costume and set designers, choreographers, writers and arrangers etc, etc. In short, what we used to have at MGM. Well, it's no longer possible. The economics of the business have killed all that. It's all too easy to ridicule Fox for spending all that money making *Dolly* but they took a brave stand – they had spent so much getting hold of the property that they wanted to turn it into a whale of a good show. It takes guts to make that kind of decision, and as the director I was excited by the challenge of blowing it up into a big and exciting picture. I'm not sorry I did it.'

One person was certainly sorry that he made *Hello, Dolly!* and that was Walter Matthau who retains the battle scars to this day. As therapy after his heart attack he had begun to take long walks and during location filming in New York he would often walk for up to five miles a day. It was one of the only ways he could keep sane. *Dolly* may have made him pause for a second and reconsider his intention of making movies as 'retirement acting'; no one needed this much aggravation in retirement. Occasionally when an interviewer would tease him with the question, 'Would you work with Barbra Streisand again?', he would rasp, 'I'd love to work with Barbra Streisand again, in something appropriate. Perhaps Macbeth!'

Chapter Eight

With the 'absolute nightmare' of *Hello, Dolly!* fast receding into memory, Matthau moved on to the happier professional chore of filming *Cactus Flower*. Billy Wilder's frequent scriptwriting partner I.A.L. Diamond had adapted the Abe Burrows Broadway hit which had been distilled from a French farce. When forties' wonder-director Preston Sturges was once asked what was the message of his films, he dryly replied, 'No message, just a gentle massage.' *Cactus Flower* falls into the category of being a 'gentle massage'.

Matthau was cast as prosperous, middle-aged bachelor dentist Julian Winston, free from any ties and determined to stay that way. His professional life is smoothly organised by his business-like secretary Stephanie (Ingrid Bergman) and his private needs are administered to by his mistress, the considerably younger, cookie Toni (Goldie Hawn) who lives in Greenwich village. Toni believes that Julian is married with a family and, in despair, she attempts suicide, only to be rescued by her neighbour Igor (Rick Lenz). Shocked at what his deception has led to Julian proposes marriage but Toni has no desire to be a home-breaker. Julian is forced to invent an unfaithful wife and her lover to assuage any feeling of guilt on

Toni's part. In desperation he turns to Stephanie who is delighted to pretend to be Mrs Winston, a role she has long wanted to play for real. Seizing the once-in-a-lifetime opportunity she blossoms forth and is revealed in Julian's eyes as a lovely, funny woman and ideal partner for life. Toni realises this too when she sees them together and Mr and Mrs Winston decide not to be parted.

On Broadway Lauren Bacall had triumphed as the long-neglected, frumpy secretary who reveals her true personality and Barry Nelson had complemented her as the dentist. Producer Mike Frankovich acquired the film rights to *Cactus Flower* and signed Matthau to play Winston and Goldie Hawn, in her first major film role, as his young playmate. The actress he had in mind to play Stephanie was Ingrid Bergman who was reluctant to accept the part. She had already refused an opportunity to take the play to London and felt that, at fifty-four, she was a little long in the tooth to play a thirty-five year old dental secretary. Frankovich flew to Paris with the film's director Gene Saks and was completely enchanted by the radiant, youthful Bergman who gave in to his entreaties and agreed to fly to Hollywood for her first film there in twenty years. The only person not entirely happy with the decision was Lauren Bacall, slightly upset to be passed over in favour of a woman ten years her senior. But there was no lasting hostility and soon afterwards the two actresses would become firm and lasting friends.

In Bergman's autobiography Frankovich recalled, 'Walter Matthau is notoriously unimpressionable. But just before Ingrid arrived, he looked very worried and kept nagging me, "How do you think we will get on? Will she like me?" Ingrid loved him. The three of them, Ingrid, Goldie and Walter got on like a house on fire.

And at the end of the film Goldie said, "Oh, but she's a woman's woman. I mean, she's everything a woman should be. She's the kind of woman men aren't afraid of because she's so warm. I thought I'd be awfully intimidated by her, so intimidated I wouldn't be able to function. It wasn't that way at all. I didn't feel I had to compete. I just felt privileged to be in the same picture with her."'

Matthau enjoyed working with her too and the company had as much fun as the audience did when the film was released. Bergman surrendered herself to the comic masters on the production, joking in a letter to her husband, 'I think Gene Saks, the director, is very thankful for all the good advice I'm giving him as – as usual – I interfere with his direction. The only real sourpuss is the poor author, I.A.L. Diamond, because I try to make them cut all his jokes which I don't find all that funny. So far I haven't succeeded, and don't think I will, because as we sat round the table at the read-through everybody was falling over laughing. I knew then that I was lost . . .'

Not entirely convincing as a mousey, unattractive secretary, Bergman was nevertheless delightful in one of her all too rare comic roles, Goldie Hawn won an Oscar as the Best Supporting Actress of 1969 and the film's box-office takings were somewhere in excess of eleven million dollars. The *New York Times* believed that, 'the teaming of Matthau with the ultra-feminine Miss Bergman, in a rare comedy venture, was inspirational on somebody's part . . . the two stars mesh perfectly.' In Britain the *Evening Standard* applauded Matthau as, 'a character who can smirk lechery as if a baked potato were in either cheek'.

By now Matthau's comic prowess was a byword in the business, his perfect timing and lugubrious features could enhance any material and his professionalism went without saying. He had reached a stage in his career where he could choose his roles. It was at this time that he decided to move permanently to the West Coast; the California climate was good for his health and that's where the work was. He calls acting for the cinema 'Retirement acting – you just give an exhibition of your former skills. Films are piecework. You do a little job. Then you do it over and over again. You don't even have to learn your lines – you do so many rehearsals, you learn them on set.' His oft-voiced disdain for the demands of the medium emerged from his earliest experiences in the film capital during the fifties. 'I realised that directors in movies have virtually no idea of characterisation. They're cutters, technicians, people from families who are big in the business. You'd come in, no one would even introduce you to anyone, you'd start the most intimate kind of scene and you didn't know the person. So I started asking questions, holding the whole schedule up. I had to do that to get noticed, in order for them to say, "there's that pain in the ass actor who wants to know who he is, where he's coming from and why he's saying the lines . . . one of those artistic actors".'

In California the Matthaus began by renting a house from Paul Newman and Joanne Woodward. 'The rent was three thousand seven hundred dollars a month. One month's rent in that place was more than my family paid in twenty years' rent down on the lower East side in New York.' They quickly purchased their own house in the Pacific Palisades area and moved in, equally quickly involving themselves in the thick of the Hollywood social scene. Socialising didn't come easy to a man with a heart condition who describes himself as 'Olympic shy'. He has revealed, 'It's an on-going dilemma for me but I can't afford to show it. You have to be vulnerable to be a good actor but if you're too vulnerable you can't do it. I hate parties. My wife says, "I think we ought to go", so we go. When I get there I crack jokes. There is a social obligation to participate rather than just sitting by the wall but I'm not a social person. I've overcome my shyness with a façade of professional horseshit.'

Carol is known as one of the most social women in town, which necessitates some compromising in their private life. 'She's the most social woman in the world. In fact, the lowest name in her address book is the Queen of Rumania. It does make life a bit awkward. I make an effort, none the less, it doesn't alter the fact that given a chance I'd rather stay at home with a good book.'

In 1970, as an indication of his growing popularity, Matthau made his first appearance in the poll of top ten box-office stars in America. He slipped in at the number ten position, his good friend Jack Lemmon was eighth and his not-so-good friend Barbra Streisand was ninth. The following year he reached his highest ever position of number seven, Lemmon was number twenty-three that year and Streisand sixteenth. At the age of fifty he was at the peak of his commercial standing, command-ing a fee of half a million dollars and ten per cent of a film's gross. Ironically, Burt Lancaster and Kirk Douglas, the stars of Matthau's first films, were said to be unbankable for any project with a budget over two million dollars, at least according to *Playboy* magazine. Characteristically, Matthau used his status to facilitate the making of two films which might otherwise never have happened and, in the process, helped Jack Lemmon realise a lifetime's ambition.

The first of these two films he made with Elaine May, a successful cabaret performer who had entered the world of cinema in 1967, acting opposite Jack Lemmon in *Luv*.

She had then written a screenplay entitled *A New Leaf*, based on a short story, *The Green Heart* by Jack Ritchie, which she also wanted to direct. Matthau was attracted to the project, and his name on a contract ensured that Paramount would allow her to realise her ambition.

After only a few weeks of filming on *A New Leaf* it was obvious that all was not well. As Matthau explained, 'Within two weeks Miss May had fired everybody. She said she'd have fired me only I was already too established in the picture – but she is one of the most delightful and talented ladies I have ever worked with.' Delightful and talented she may have been but quick-working she wasn't. During production it wasn't unusual for no cameras to start rolling until four in the afternoon. Paramount executives were well aware that time means money and wanted to know what was going on. They can't have been overjoyed when May informed them, 'You see, Walter chases me around all day in an attempt to grab my body and by four pm he's tired out and we're ready to shoot.' Attempting to calm the troubled waters Matthau reported, 'The reason she starts so late is that she's a bit uncertain and she likes to rehearse a lot. Don't worry – the picture will only cost three or four million and you'll learn a lot about the business, about artists. Chalk it up to experience.'

One worry for Matthau was the water-logged ending envisaged for the picture, as Stanley Jaffe, then head of Paramount, recalled: 'We had a lot of problems on *New Leaf* and the last sixteen pages of the script took place as the couple are shooting the rapids on the river. Walter came up to me and explained that he'd had a heart attack and that we'd better get a double because he wasn't going in the water. He suggested we could perhaps shoot the double from the back and that if he were to go in the water a wet suit would close up his pores and leave him freezing cold. Come the actual day of filming, the assistant director came running up to me and said, "Can you please get Walter out of the water?" When I arrived on the scene, he had put on a wet suit and found almost a whirlpool in the water and was spinning around like a twelve-year-old in a tub. We couldn't keep him out of the water!'

On the set of *A New Leaf* the publicity-assistant asked Matthau how much he was enjoying his belated star status and wasn't all the public recognition that he now received what made it all worthwhile for an actor? 'Hell no. My gratification came years ago from the critics and my colleagues,' he replied. 'When they say a guy becomes a star and hasn't changed, what they really mean is that he hasn't let the outside change in relation to him. I simply don't succumb to it. This morning we were doing a street scene for *A New Leaf* and one of those tourists asked if I'd pose. I said no. The guy says, "Whaddya mean, can't I take your picture?" I said, "Sure you can. But I won't pose. The monkey house is to the left, around the corner."'

Matthau might well have welcomed some instant recognition when he went shopping in New York during the filming of *A New Leaf*. Casually dressed in baggy pants, torn sneakers and a sweatshirt he walked into a pricey delicatessen and asked the price of sturgeon, a not unreasonable enquiry. The shop assistant gave him the once over and then proceeded to ignore the actor in favour of another customer. Irritated Matthau repeated his question. The salesman turned on him and announced, 'Six dollars a pound.' With perfect timing Matthau retorted, 'I'll take a hundred pounds.'

In *A New Leaf* Matthau plays a wealthy New York bachelor Henry Graham who lives an expensive, spendthrift life. One day the money runs out and, thunderstruck, he faces the awesome prospect of poverty. His butler suggests the perfect solution – marriage to a suitably wealthy partner. Graham takes the suggestion one step further and plots murder. Fortunately for him, he stumbles over Henrietta Lowell (May), a socially graceless botanist worth a small fortune, who has no relatives. Grimly determined, he sets out to win her hand despite the fact he finds her, 'so clumsy she has to be vacuumed every time she eats'.

Armed with a copy of *The Beginners Guide to Toxicology* he spends their honeymoon plotting her demise whilst she discovers a new species of fern which she names after him. Later, on a field trip the perfect opportunity for his plans arises when the couple hit a dangerous set of rapids and Henrietta struggles helplessly against the current. However, he discovers that he cannot allow her to drown and rescues her instead. Struggling ashore she enquires, 'I'll always be able to depend on you, won't I Henry?' 'I'm afraid so,' he answers.

Sentimental the film may have been but *A New Leaf* is an extremely agreeable throwback to the screwball situation comedies of the thirties with May's Henrietta an unforgettable, totally dependent mess and Matthau, cast against type as the playboy, incisive and observant in his playing. Grossing some fifteen million dollars *A New Leaf* was one of Matthau's biggest successes. But Elaine May, unhappy with the final result, and disagreeing with Paramount's handling of her work, sued the studio, claiming in her suit: 'The film has been changed from a comedy suspense story to a cliché-ridden, banal story. Totally new scenes have been constructed, large parts of the story have been omitted. Nearly every line of dialogue is out of context, with the result that the film being released is in no way the plaintiff's.' She claimed damages of $150,000 and the case was settled out of court. She has not directed for the cinema since.

Before playing his second hunch, in which Jack Lemmon became involved, Matthau had signed up for a reunion with the writing talents of Neil Simon on *Plaza Suite*. The schedule for the film allowed for two weeks in New York and six weeks at Paramount Studios in California. The film provided Matthau with the challenge of three characterisations in three separate stories within one film. On stage George C. Scott and Maureen Stapleton had amply filled three roles a piece. However, when it came to the film, it was deemed more appropriate to restrict an actor to one role and Matthau was approached to play one of the characters. He asked for a one million dollar fee. Maureen Stapleton was retained from the stage production and Lee Grant and Barbara Harris were enlisted for the other female roles. Then, after a change of heart, Matthau was contracted for all the male leads although there was still to be a different leading lady for each segment. His actual salary was $100,000 plus a participation in the profits.

Plaza Suite takes place in Suite 719 of the Plaza Hotel in New York City. In nostalgic mood Karen Nash (Maureen Stapleton) returns to the spot where, twenty-four years ago to the day, she spent her honeymoon with husband Sam (Matthau). Their marriage has gone a little sour and Karen sees this as a romantic opportunity to start again. When Sam arrives he explains that she is a day early in celebrating their anniversary, that it is only twenty-three years since their honeymoon and that they spent it in Suite 819. He produces some work which he has brought with him and suggests she might like to go to the theatre, alone. Discussing their problems, Sam admits to having an affair with his secretary, which is what Karen had feared, 'You were working three nights a week; we weren't getting any richer.' Sam leaves to meet his secretary and Karen is left alone with her planned champagne celebration.

Originally, Simon planned to use this story as the complete plot for his play, 'But when the husband walks out and the waiter comes in with their order and says, "Is he coming back?" and the wife looks after him and says, "Funny you should ask that", there's no point in going on. That's the end of the play! What to do now? So, I thought of the concept of putting other actors into the same set.' The other two acts in the film involved Matthau as Jesse Kiplinger, a Hollywood producer, using Suite 719 to seduce an old girlfriend, Muriel Tate (Barbara Harris), from his hometown of Tenafly, New Jersey; and as Roy Hubley, an anxious father who has spent a fortune on his daughter Mimsey's (Jenny Sullivan) wedding at the Plaza Hotel. Mimsey has locked herself in suite 719, afraid that she and her fiancé will become as quarrelsome as her parents. Roy and his wife Norma (Lee Grant) lay siege to the room to no avail, but Mimsey finally emerges when her fiancé Borden (Tom Carey) tells her to, 'cool it!' The happy couple ride into the sunset on a motorbike with Roy moaning, 'She was better off in the bathroom, ya hear me? Better off in the bathroom.'

Unfortunately, *Plaza Suite* reveals its stage origins rather too much to be an entirely successful film. In an interview with *Time* magazine Matthau explained his mental pictures behind the trio of characterisations: 'That first guy now, he had a Jewish father and an Italian mother, grew up poor and got rich in the garment business. The second guy is half Jewish and half German, grew up in Tenafly, New Jersey. The third guy, he was raised on tenth avenue in Hell's Kitchen. Worked on the docks, eventually got a good job in the union and saved a lot of money for his daughter's wedding. He's Irish, German and Swedish.'

As a display of Matthau's versatility, *Plaza Suite* works well enough, although the second segment is rather weak. Simon himself at one time regarded it as the worst film that had been made of one of his plays. 'I was very unhappy about it. I didn't like the cast. I didn't like the picture,' he says. 'There were a couple of moments . . . but I know it could have been done infinitely better. I would only have used Walter in the last sequence, and probably Lee Grant. I think Walter Matthau was wrong to play all three parts. That's a trick Peter Sellers can do. I have to accept some of the blame for the film. I kept all the action in one room. It was rather confining, we could have gone into other suites. I didn't think it out, but I learned from that.'

If Elaine May had had more than her share of problems as a first time director even Jack Lemmon, with his reputation and track record, encountered enormous obstacles when he came to make his directorial début with *Kotch*.

Some years previously Lemmon's press agent Richard Carter had read a book by Katharine Topkins, enjoyed the slightly sentimental tale of an old man's quest for dignity, and made his bid for the film rights. He gained an option on the book and commissioned writer John Paxton to write the script. Paxton's earlier film credits included *On the Beach* (1959) and *The Wild One* (1953). The material was originally planned as a vehicle for Spencer Tracy. When Tracy died in 1967 Carter had decided to change his approach to the project and began to search instead for a director whose name would guarantee finance for his first film as a producer. Among those approached, without success, were Mike Nichols, Paul Newman and Arthur Penn.

In February 1969 Carter decided to ask Lemmon for his professional opinion on the *Kotch* script, as he later explained in a biography of Lemmon: 'I sent a copy of the script to Jack more as a courtesy than anything else, just to let him know what I was moonlighting on. A couple of weeks later he called, wanting to talk to me about *Kotch*. My first thought was, "Oh, my God, he wants to play it!" I wondered how the hell we could ever make him look like a seventy-six-year-old guy. At the same time I was thinking of what he could bring to that part with his great sense of timing.'

Lemmon however didn't want to act in *Kotch*. He had fallen in love with the script and wondered if there was the remotest chance he could be considered as the director. 'A strange thing happened to me when I was reading the script,' he said. 'From the very beginning I could visualise the scenes depicting the relationship between the old man and his grandson. Throughout the rest of the script, the scenes were playing in my mind, just as though they were on the screen.

'I must say I was walloped by the story. There was nothing in it for me to play: I think it would have been wrong for me to try to play the old man. After I finished reading the script, I thought it over. I said to Dick, "I love it. When you start making a list of directors put me among them."' Carter hadn't even thought of Lemmon as the director but was immediately struck by the idea and jumped at the actor's suggestion.

Lemmon further analysed his reasons for wanting to do *Kotch*: 'I was drawn to *Kotch* first by the character and the individual spirit of the human being. I was fascinated by it.

'It raises a lot of questions that I think need to be raised, but I was not trying to make any kind of statement about old age. I merely wanted to do a nice little drama about a character who happens to be old.

'What do you do if you're seventy-five-years old but young from the neck up? That's what troubles Kotch.'

Among the obstacles faced by the Lemmon-Carter team were financing and casting. *Kotch* is a gentle, disarming comedy which says something about people within a dramatic context and has a lead character in his seventies. To the extremely youth-orientated corporate mind of Hollywood the project was a definite no-go in commercial terms. Among the actors mentioned for the role of septuagenarian Joseph P. Kotch was James Cagney, Lemmon's old captain from *Mister Roberts*, and Cary Grant, but both chose to remain in retirement. Lemmon's first choice for the part was distinguished veteran Fredric March. Alas March was not really in good enough health to manage the demands of a leading role and the studios probably considered him a poor insurance risk who was past being a top box-office draw. Whatever their reasons no one was willing to finance *Kotch*.

One day, when it appeared that the film would never be made, Lemmon received an unexpected phone call from Matthau who said, 'If you haven't cast that part of the old man yet would you tell them about me? I'd like to do it.' Lemmon and Carter had even discussed the possibility of Matthau playing Kotcher but didn't really entertain the notion of someone twenty-five years younger being that interested in the part. When Matthau himself made the approach the idea seemed one of the best they'd heard in a long while. When Fredric March gracefully bowed out of the package, Matthau was accepted. It was one of the rare occasions when he had expressed interest in a part without having read the script. Carol had read it and been so impressed that she broke her vow of silence about voicing opinions on her husband's career and cajolled Matthau into making the call.

Even with the services of two Oscar-winning, seemingly highly bankable stars it was still difficult to find a backer for *Kotch*. Eventually a deal was struck with Martin Baum of ABC pictures for a budget that could flatteringly be termed 'competitive' – one million six hundred thousand dollars. With such slim pickings, frugality was the order of the day and Lemmon called on the services of his closest colleagues and friends. Lemmon's wife, actress Felicia Farr, was cast as Kotcher's daughter-in-law Wilma and Matthau's stepdaughter Lucy, from Carol's marriage to William Saroyan, was also enlisted.

During production the Lemmon-Matthau team found that it could work just as smoothly with one member of the duo behind the camera. Filming finished at 5.59pm on the forty-fifth day of a forty-five day schedule and $15,000 under budget.

The couple could joke that on the first day of filming Lemmon approached Matthau, to be met with a reproachful stare and the question, 'You're not going to tell me how to act are you?' Lemmon admitted, 'We respect each other and we know each other's reactions. I could anticipate how Walter would react, both as an actor and as a human being. I could say half a sentence to him and he'd say, "Gotcha". It's the same kind of relationship that Walter and I have with Billy Wilder.

'Some actors think only of themselves. Not Walter. He's not that kind of scene-stealer who wants to give a bravura performance and will do anything to get his little bitty shtick across. He thinks about his own performance, but he tries to help other actors as well.

'He and I are similar in our approach to acting. We realise that it is harder to play good material, because there are so many ways you can do it. Bad scripts are easy; there's usually only one way to do them. Walter will take direction well, I found, unless something goes totally against his instincts. But I directed him mostly by leaving him alone. He's so inventive that when I was editing the film, I found he never did the same thing twice, and I wanted to kill him because it was almost impossible to cut.'

Matthau, with a choice role and a friend behind the camera, knew he was experiencing the film-making process at its most rewarding and claimed that Lemmon was 'a fantastic director because he has a most unique ability to communicate with the broad spectrum of personalities on the scene, a man with a magnificent command of all the integral parts of a script.

'He has taste, talent and imagination. And being an actor, he has the added advantage of understanding an actor's problems.'

J. P. Kotcher is a physically-fit, mentally alert seventy-two-year-old whose liveliness, constant stream of anecdotes and wise advice has become irritating to his family. His daughter-in-law wants to pack him off to an old folks' home and displays her lack of faith in 'Kotch' by hiring a babysitter, Erica (Deborah Winters) to take care of her young son. Erica is more interested in the use of the family sofa with her boyfriend than the needs of the child and is fired. Unmarried, pregnant and alone Erica leaves school and the neighbourhood. Kotch decides to follow her and help her through the pregnancy.

Invigorated by his newfound responsibility Kotch develops a wary friendship with Erica and an understanding that crosses the generations. When the child is born Kotch is again on his own but the tender memory of the episode helps him to be reconciled into his family.

Lemmon found the character of Kotch strongly reminiscent of his father, while Matthau based his understanding of Kotch on a judge he had known in New York who was in his eighties, never wore a coat even when it was below zero and walked very erect, unlike Matthau who tends to slouch. The character is multi-dimensional and Matthau doesn't shy away from displaying the irascibility of the man and the thick-skinned eccentricity which would not exactly endear him to his nearest and dearest. The film also allowed Matthau to bring out the pathos in the character, while making some fine judgements to avoid the mawkish sloppiness lurking around every corner in this kind of film. A syrupy musical score, including a theme song 'Life is What You Make It', tended to work against the efforts of the actors to avoid the lachrymose and the finished film didn't escape some negative reviews. Matthau received excellent personal notices. In *New York* magazine Judith Crist wrote, 'Small doubt that *Kotch* is sentimental, but with Walter Matthau in the title role and Jack Lemmon making a most auspicious directorial début, the charm predominates and the result is nice, neat and touching.

'Matthau, refreshingly non-star and totally in character right down to the teeth-sucking tics of senility shows a new dimension to his art.'

The efforts of everyone involved were rewarded by the overwhelmingly positive response of the public. At the film's first preview in San Diego the audience gave it a standing ovation and the cinema manager reported that it was the first time in the theatre's history that no one emerged to buy popcorn, 'or even to go to the john'. The film received four Oscar nominations including one as Best Song for 'Life is What You Make It' with music by Marvin Hamlisch and lyrics by Alan and Marilyn

Bergman, Matthau's first nomination as Best Actor and two further nominations in the minor categories. Matthau's fellow nominees were Gene Hackman for *The French Connection*, Peter Finch for *Sunday, Bloody Sunday*, the previous year's winner George C. Scott for *The Hospital* and Topol for *Fiddler on the Roof*.

Lemmon and Matthau were both present at the awards ceremony on 10 April 1972 at the Dorothy Chandler Pavilion in Los Angeles. A special Oscar was presented to Charlie Chaplin on his return to Hollywood for the first time in twenty years. Carol had been a room-mate of Oona Chaplin at one stage and the two had remained friends. Matthau, sporting a moustache for the filming of *Pete'n'Tillie*, was on hand to present the Best Actress Award to Jane Fonda for *Klute*. Traditionally this task would have fallen to the previous year's winner of the Best Actor Award but Matthau explained that the tradition would be broken with that year, 'due to circumstances beyond our control'. George C. Scott was hardly likely to appear on the Academy's behalf after rejecting his Oscar for *Patton*.

In the event *Kotch* didn't win any awards; Gene Hackman was deemed to have given the best performance by an actor in 1971. No one enjoys losing but Matthau can't have minded too much – there would be other chances. For Lemmon any added recognition would have been the frosting on the cake. After all, *Kotch* remained Lemmon's 'single, unbelievably, most exciting and gratifying experience of my life. There has been nothing like it, nothing to approach it, in any way, both personally and professionally.'

Chapter Nine

Pete'n'Tillie marked Matthau's first professional association with both his co-star, comedienne Carol Burnett, and the film's director, Martin Ritt. Burnett was returning to the screen for the first time in nine years, after building a reputation as one of television's top funny ladies. Ritt is one of Hollywood's foremost dealers in heavyweight material with a list of credits ranging from *Edge of the City* in 1956 to *The Great White Hope* in 1970, stopping along the way for the Oscar-winning *Hud* (1963), *The Spy Who Came in From the Cold* (1965) and *The Molly Maguires* (1969). He also enjoyed the status of one of the best tipsters in Hollywood.

Still a dedicated gambling man, though no longer with the fever of one possessed, Matthau would often gravitate towards a racetrack on his days off, usually with a friend in tow. 'I have dragged Billy Wilder out to the racetrack many times. He hates horse racing. I love to go to the races. Will go every afternoon unless work interferes. The thing about a track is there is a long pause between races, you know, fifteen, twenty minutes, and Billy can't stand it. But I love this. Billy is not a gambler. You see, it's the time between races that gets a gambler going. You study your form sheets. You walk around trying to get some inside dope. You go to the clubhouse, look the horses over. Best of all, you try to run into Marty Ritt. Ritt you cannot call a gambler. He wins too many bets. He always has the edge.'

Based on a novella called *Witch's Milk* by Peter De Vries, *Pete'n'Tillie* splits into two parts; the first a witty, sympathetically-drawn account of the courtship between two mature adults, well over the age of twenty-one; and the second, a stark change of gear, when, as a married couple, they face the illness and death of their only child. Matthau as Pete is a sleepily witty bachelor who offers the spinsterish Tillie the prospect of coming up to his place for, 'a spot of heavy breathing'. Tillie philosophically reckons, 'When you've reached my age, and your friends are beginning to worry about you, blind dates are a way of life.'

The Oscar-nominated screenplay by veteran Julius J. Epstein also offered more than one-dimensional supporting roles to Geraldine Page and Rene Auberjonois. Page plays Gertrude, a woman of very indeterminate age who is Tillie's close friend with a sideline in matchmaking. Auberjonois is Jimmy Twitchell, a homosexual acquaintance who makes a touching proposal to Tillie when it appears that the trauma of her son's death means the end of her marriage to Pete. While the film never totally shoulders the burden of its mood change from comedy to stark drama it is a civilised, compassionate entertainment, containing more than a few home truths about the human condition. For Matthau it delivered a welcome, if slightly offbeat, change of pace and another success. With a gross figure of some nine million dollars, *Pete'n'Tillie* was amongst the top twenty films on release in America throughout 1973.

Asked to describe working with Walter Matthau, Carol Burnett said, 'He was an absolute delight and a professional in every sense of the word.' It was a feeling reciprocated by Matthau who gained a particular satisfaction in having a working partner who was also a specialist in laughter. 'We're a couple of movie clowns', he explained on set. 'We worked overtime to make each other laugh.

'I wouldn't have dreamed of trying it on some of my leading ladies like Felicia Farr, Maureen Stapleton, Barbra Streisand and Ingrid Bergman, but with Carol Burnett or Lucille Ball or any other comedienne, yes! It's a showbusiness compulsion.

'I broke up Carol every chance I got during filming. I let up when we got to our dramatic scenes, of course. That wouldn't have been fair. But whenever we went back to comedy, I had to make her bust out laughing in the middle of a speech.'

The mood of having fun while working wasn't a one-sided affair either; Burnett could give just as good as she got, as Matthau discovered. 'I didn't know how she would play the seduction scene. I knew she wouldn't be nude – that's not Carol – but that there would have to be a suggestion of nudity. Well, I thought it would be a body stocking. Comes the moment for Carol to arrive from her dressing room. Director Martin Ritt has charitably closed the set. I am getting goose-bumps from lack of clothing. Carol, I see, is wearing a covering robe. We get ready to do the scene. I remove her robe and do a double-take. She has been fitted with an enormous bra stuffed with bean bags. The sight of her in that trick get-up destroyed me.

'She had her revenge. I couldn't stop laughing. And I broke up even when she came back to do the scene the way it was written.'

Matthau, who has always prided himself on the general quality of his film and stage roles, was beginning to realise that stardom, while it is every performer's dream, also has its drawbacks. Firstly, having attained a certain stature in the business, making the right decisions from among the scripts offered becomes very important. It is no longer possible to be an undiscriminating, non-stop worker, keeping the finances in credit and bankrolling the betting. Careful decisions are necessary to stay at the top. The other problem with stardom is the way in which a performer can slowly become trapped in a mould. He or she has become a star through being considered especially talented at doing a certain thing – embodying the strong, silent Western hero myth or being an expert light comedy actor. The danger then is that the star will become pigeonholed and his career will not progress. If he has a penchant for comedy, film companies, which after all need to make commercial films will offer him all the comedies going and nothing else. Matthau, at this stage, realised the possibility of being trapped into replicating a certain type of performance ad infinitum and wanted to avoid it. While playing comedy has fulfilments and rewards it is only one facet of his prodigious talent.

Matthau has his own theory on the way the audience is treated by the film executives. The executives, he believes, are guided by a purely commercial instinct. 'I always think of an old story about a man sitting in the doorway with his old hound dog. Another old man comes up to him with a bag of candy. The second old man says, "That's a mighty fine dog of yours. Would he like some candy?" The first man replies, "Well, he eats garbage, so maybe he'd like candy."

'The moral is that the public only gets garbage when that's all it can get. I try to make the candy pictures. I believe there are enough people with tastes like my own to make it pay off."

Candy pictures aside, Matthau was now looking for

something with a hard centre and wasn't finding the task easy. For his serious turn he eventually settled on the ingeniously plotted thriller, *Charley Varrick*, and the dour police drama, *The Laughing Policeman*, known in Britain as *An Investigation of Murder*. In the case of *Charley Varrick* he was somewhat less than impressed. 'It was a poor script. I was looking for something non-domestic but after reading a few pages, I threw the manuscript in the fire. Then the producers asked for it back. I couldn't return it so Don Siegel came around to ask me why I'd burned it. "Could you get me another copy?" I asked. Then I showed him, every page I showed him. It was junk. When I was making it I came in every day and asked for thirty-five changes. At the end it was still junk.'

Matthau's attitude to *Charley Varrick* is hard to fathom as Don Siegel's film, from a novel *The Looters* by John Reese, was a slickly-paced, superior thriller with the many deft touches one would expect from someone with proven ability in the field. A former editor, Siegel had been making films since the forties with notable successes in *Riot in Cell Block Eleven* (1954) and *Invasion of the Bodysnatchers* (1956). A fruitful collaboration with Clint Eastwood on *Coogan's Bluff* (1968) and *Dirty Harry* (1971), among others, had brought his name to the forefront of the public's attention and *Charley Varrick* is simply, if rather pretentiously, billed as 'A Siegel Film'.

Charley Varrick (Matthau), a former stunt pilot and now a crop-duster, supplements his income with the occasional, modestly-budgeted small bank robbery. The take averages between $10,000 and $15,000 and police interest is short-lived. On one such occasion, in the western town of Tres Cruces, everything that can go wrong does. Two policemen interrupt the proceedings, resulting in the death of Charley's wife, his accomplice, a bank guard and a policeman.

Back at their hideaway Varrick and his partner Harman Sullivan (Andy Robinson) discover a much higher take than expected – $750,000. Varrick concludes (correctly) that it can only be Mafia money, which is going through a respectable laundering before departing the country. The 'mob' neither forgives nor forgets and Varrick will now be the quarry in a relentless pursuit.

Maynard Boyle (John Vernon) the bank president and front man for the Vegas mob hires Molly (Joe Don Baker) to exact revenge. Molly, a monolithic Southerner, is not someone to give up on a case. When Sullivan is killed Varrick runs for his life but is a cunning enough operator to outwit the 'mob', fool Molly by stage-managing his own death and live up to his billing as Charley Varrick, 'Last of the Independents'.

Charley Varrick is a slick, well-edited thriller with not a wholesome character in sight; there are 'good' bad guys and 'bad' bad guys but everyone is grasping, self-seeking and usually criminal. The audience is on Charley's side because he's the outsider against the system; one man against the 'mob'. Having him portrayed by Matthau helps, with his wry delivery and sardonic demeanour inflecting character and in-dividuality into an anti-hero. Among a rich gallery of performances are Sheree North's as a lady forger, Felicia Farr's as Boyle's mistress and that of a young boy played by one Charlie Matthau. As one would expect, Siegel handled the action scenes with aplomb, particularly an exciting dogfight between an aeroplane and a car in the tense climax. *Charley Varrick*, despite what Matthau believes, is a film with a lot going for it and represents one of the best syntheses of his established film character (world-weary, cynical and melancholic) in a dramatic context.

Charley Varrick was a critical hit and a modest financial

118

success. In Britain, whose acting traditions Matthau had long admired (he claims Robert Donat is his favourite actor) the Society of Film and Television Arts voted him the Best Actor of 1973, shared between *Charley Varrick* and *Pete'n'Tillie*.

Matthau's second choice to break out of his 'domestic comedy' routine was less welcomed. Filmed in San Francisco *The Laughing Policeman* was based on a novel by Per Wahloo and Maj Sjowall. A routine, if still creditable cop story, it finds Matthau as one Jake Martin, a long-serving homicide detective. The story begins when a man enters a bus, assembles a sub-machine gun from his tote bag and kills all on board – eight passengers and the driver. Martin arrives on the scene to discover that one of the victims was his partner, Evans.

Assigned a new partner, Leo Larsen (Bruce Dern), Martin begins his 'investigation of a murder'. According to the dead man's girlfriend the cop had been spending his official holiday delving into the unsolved 'Teresa' murder case of two years ago in which the mistress of a man named Camerero was found strangled. With little home life and a new partner for whom he has scant enthusiasm Martin charts his own course, following any leads through the gay bars, X-rated movie theatres and boarding houses of the city. He becomes convinced that there is a link between the 'Teresa' murder and the bus massacre and enlists the grudging support of Larsen to prove his point. Their contrasting styles combine to trap a mass murderer and clear the reputation of Evans.

At the time of *The Laughing Policeman*'s appearance the movie-going audience had become rather indifferent to the appeal of another well-crafted, sobering examination of police procedure. Raised out of the ordinary by fine location photography and an excellent cast it was still just another police story with by-the-book Dern and individualistic old-timer Matthau fated to endure a personality clash before close contact and playing the older man's hunch brings the onset of mutual respect. The film was poorly received in some quarters. In Britain, the less than charitable *Spectator* review read, 'The film is interesting for what it shows of San Francisco's undertown, but its psychology is lame, the plot an illogical mess, and Stuart Rosenberg (the director) is feebly voyeuristic in his use of drugs and homosexuality to perk up the spirits.' In America, Pauline Kael firmly put Matthau in his place for letting the audience down, writing, 'Matthau used to be a strategic scene-stealer: He used to putter around looking rumpled and sleepy while dropping zingers. This time he's as square as the squarest of actors; he does the ancient obvious, while Dern's contentious but muffled manner – the way he puts cobwebs on his lines so there's an instant's delay before you quite get the joke – is the latest in fey, ruminative one-upmanship.'

These comments must have stung, but extending your repertory to play a conventional leading role and then being met with criticism for not being your usual self is all part and parcel of stardom. Continuing the break from straight comic roles he bounced right back with *The Taking of Pelham, One Two Three*, an excellent mixture of humour and suspense. John Godey's novel on which the film was based had reached the bestseller lists and the screenplay was from the tried and tested pen of Peter Stone.

Matthau is transit-authority lieutenant Garber whose fairly humdrum chores are rudely interrupted when a subway train is hijacked in a meticulously prepared extortion plan. The train is stopped between stations, causing havoc to the whole underground system. The leader of the hijackers, Mr Blue (Robert Shaw), demands a million dollars ransom and threatens to kill one passenger for every minute the authorities are late in meeting the demand.

Garber faces the responsibility of cracking Blue's seemingly foolproof escape plan and keeping uppermost the safety of the passengers. His problems are complicated by the city's rulers who know the metropolis is broke and that they will have great difficulty coming up with the goods. The unpopular mayor has flu and can't face either the problem or the inevitable public disapproval of whatever action he takes. The cross-section of hostages, convincingly terrorised by Blue and his gang, hold their breath and pray whilst Garber plays cat and mouse with Blue, trying to anticipate his next move.

Eventually Garber and the authorities accede to the demands and move into the subway to track down the hijackers. When Blue is cornered by Garber he chooses to commit suicide on the electrified track. It appears that only Mr Green (Martin Balsam) has escaped but a simple sneeze betrays his presence to Garber in the film's closing frame.

The Taking of Pelham, One Two Three filmed for nine weeks in the Manhattan subway system, mainly at South Brooklyn's Court Street Station. The latter is now only used for making movies and training new subway crews. Matthau's character spends little time actually in the subway, but the other actors were less fortunate in having to film in an environment where the slightest movement along the track stirred up the accumulated mass of black dust. One of the actors observed that it was, 'like being in a West Virginia coal mine that was on strike'.

Well matched in his adversarial conflict with British actor Robert Shaw, Matthau turned up for filming looking like the character Stavros from the television series Kojak. Director Joseph Sargent explained: 'Walter Matthau reported to the picture with the notion that he should play his role as a curly-haired Italian. It seemed like a crutch, and Matthau is too full an actor to need a crutch.' The frizzy hair-style was quickly replaced by a slicked-down trim and a New Yorker characterisation of much-put-upon resourcefulness.

During the years since his Oscar nomination Matthau had remained within the elite twenty top box-office stars, usually placed between fifteenth and nineteenth in the list. He was working at as hard a pace as ever, even slotting in a cameo appearance in the all-star disaster film *Earthquake*, unsubtle in the manner in which he mugged his way through the part of a token drunk, tottering and gulping his way through the big 'quake. One intrepid British reporter asked the film's director Mark Robson, 'You're really into the *Airport* and *Poseidon Adventure* market with this, aren't you?' To which the director retorted, 'Well, sure as hell it's not *Cries and Whispers*.' It sure as hell wasn't, but as a cardboard exercise in making money it was obviously a success. The gimmicky Sensurround system, patterned on the rumblings of an empty stomach, picked up the Oscar for best sound. What Matthau, billed under his real name, was doing there is anybody's guess. One can only hope he was making a lot of money.

In 1974 he managed to fit in his first stage work in a long while with a revival of Sean O'Casey's fifty-year-old *Juno and the Paycock* at the Mark Taper Forum in Los Angeles. Directed by George Seaton the revival boasted a starry trio of leading players with Jack Lemmon as Joxer Daly, Maureen Stapleton as Juno and Matthau as Captain Jack Boyle, the vainglorious Paycock. 'It was fixed at a party with Jack Lemmon and Maureen

Stapleton. We all suddenly decided that we wanted to do it,' he has explained. 'Even my brother, who scarcely likes anything of mine, reckons I'm all right in O'Casey. "You were quite good in that crazy Irish thing", he said.'

Lemmon was downhearted that their joint efforts weren't captured for posterity: 'When the show closed we went to every network but no one wanted to tape it as a matter of historical record. Not even Public Broadcasting Service. Our combined names didn't amount to a dime.' The networks let slip a not-to-be-repeated opportunity. *Juno and the Paycock* represents Matthau's last stage appearance to date and he has expressed no desire to return to the boards despite a number of offers. During the run of *Juno and the Paycock* he developed a duodenal ulcer and frankly admitted that, 'I get terrified in the theatre nowadays.'

In his mid-fifties he probably wasn't enjoying his position of stardom quite as much as he should have been. His move away from straight comedies had met with mixed results and his own critical instincts told him that he had produced little with which he could claim to be satisfied. His return to stage work had left the impression that *Juno and the Paycock* was in some way a farewell, in the company of good friends, to the theatre of his early career. The lure of the healthier California life, rich pickings and sometimes rewarding outcome of his 'retirement acting' for the movies had established their dominant hold. It is apparent that, with the odd exception, he had begun to cut back on his filming commitments, limiting himself to one film a year from the mid-seventies onwards.

To round off 1974 there was the enticing prospect of a film with Jack Lemmon for Billy Wilder, the first time the trio had worked together since *The Fortune Cookie*. In the interim Lemmon and Matthau had flourished, the latter reaching fully-fledged stardom, the former making his praiseworthy directorial début on *Kotch* and winning that elusive Best Actor Oscar for *Save the Tiger* (1973). For Wilder, events had not proved so glorious; it was almost as if he were being repaid for all the years of film hits and awards by hitting a period when nothing seemed to work at all. Following *The Fortune Cookie* he had worked on a number of aborted projects, not filming again until *The Private Life of Sherlock Holmes* (1970) which, drastically cut, had flopped. Two years later he produced the modestly successful *Avanti!*, one of his best productions and a film that deserved to do better. Lemmon had starred in the bittersweet romantic comedy *Avanti!* opposite Juliet Mills in her worthiest cinematic outing. Matthau would have been included in the cast as well except that there wasn't really a third role to match his status. At this stage in his lengthy career Wilder was looking for a big, fat hit to regain his respect as a box-office winner. Matthau and Lemmon were delighted to provide it.

Joseph Mankiewicz, the writer-director of some of Hollywood's most literate films, including *All About Eve* (1950), had been approached to direct a new version of the classic Broadway comedy *The Front Page*. First filmed in 1930 with Pat O'Brien and Adolphe Menjou in the star roles the film had already been remade in 1940 as *His Girl Friday* with Rosalind Russell and Cary Grant. Mankiewicz declined the offer but Universal producer Jennings Lang agreed to the suggestion of Lemmon and Matthau that they would co-star if Billy Wilder was engaged to write and direct.

It was claimed that sixty per cent of the dialogue in the Wilder-I.A.L. Diamond *Front Page* script was original, and there is certainly an unpleasant element of crudity and coarseness in the work, replacing the wit and sophistication one might have expected. In some way Wilder was hedging his bets with vulgarity to temper the material to a seventies audience; an understandable reaction from a man disappointed that more people didn't go and see his Lubitsch-style *Avanti!* 'You are not going to buck audiences at two or three million dollars a clip,' Wilder stated. 'What good is it being a marvellous composer of polkas if nobody dances the polka anymore?' If *The Front Page* ultimately disappoints it is because one expects so much of the talents involved; more than a roughneck, freewheeling, uneven farce; nevertheless it was still one of the best comedies of 1974.

Set in the press room of the Criminal Court Buildings in twenties Chicago, *The Front Page* revolves around a group of reporters – men with newsprint in their blood. They are assembled to await a hanging the next morning. One regular who expects to be absent is Hildy Johnson (Lemmon) who has decided that he is leaving the profession to marry and settle into something more respectable. This notion is sadly misguided. His editor Walter Burns (Matthau) is determined, by fair means or foul, to ensure that Hildy remains wed to his typewriter.

Visiting the press room for a farewell drink with the boys, Hildy is hooked all over again. The prisoner Earl Williams (Austin Pendleton) has escaped and only Hildy knows where he is. Burns senses a scoop and is not about to let it slip by on the flimsy excuse of a man's wedding. A myriad of complications ensue, involving Mollie Malloy (Carol Burnett) a tart who falls for Williams, the exposing of a crooked mayor and a mad scramble to ensure that Burns triumphs and retains Hildy to write 'the hottest story since the Chicago fire'.

The four-million-dollar production of *The Front Page* doesn't fire on all cylinders and Carol Burnett's performance is curiously misjudged but Lemmon and

Matthau are an incomparable double-act and their tightly-packaged interplay ensured the film success on its American release for the Christmas season of 1974.

'They are totally ideal and, in fact, I don't think it could or should have been made with others than the Odd Couple of Lemmon and Matthau,' Wilder declared. 'It is peculiar how the two, who are great personal friends of each other, and of mine, should have stuck together since that picture which they made with me. I always found that many of the best pictures made in Hollywood were love stories between men. By that I mean a teaming of Clark Gable and Spencer Tracy, of Abbott and Costello, and Laurel and Hardy, and just lately Newman and Redford. These are the great love stories; it was never Clark Gable and Joan Crawford, it is two men against each other, and I don't mean anything homosexual there.'

Matthau's role of the ogre editor who makes the newspaper world his life is tailor-made for him. In the screenplay he is described as operating, 'in the great tradition of Machiavelli, Rasputin and Count Dracula'. Matthau's beady eyes pop and swivel with gimlet joy at every dirty trick and double-cross that advances his cause. 'I always play Wilder. Wilder sees me as Wilder – a lovable rogue full of razor blades,' the actor believed, and he still had a carp or two about Wilder's straight-laced approach to directing. 'To Wilder actors are a necessary evil. I think he wishes there were some way he could make pictures without actors. He once told me that he envied Walt Disney. Donald Duck and Mickey Mouse didn't make trouble.'

To say that the film is stolen by Austin Pendleton as the pathetic, victimised communist with a head cold and a touching vulnerability is not to belittle the considerable skill of the lead performers. Continuing his analysis of the Lemmon-Matthau team Wilder said, 'Matthau is the more interesting case. After all Lemmon is attractive in his way, and a born comedian, but Matthau has little pig eyes and a nose like a pickle. But suddenly he springs to life and is absolutely magnetic. Somehow you don't expect a star to look like Matthau. He's the first of the unheroic looking actors to become really important. The curious thing is that women find Matthau very sexy. Along with Redford and Newman, suddenly on the outside and gaining, is Matthau!'

Kotch (1971), an Oscar-nominated role in a film directed by Jack Lemmon

Pete 'n' Tillie (1972) with Carol Burnett and James McAllister

Charley Varrick (1973) with the film's director, Don Siegel

The Front Page (1974) with his favourite director, Billy Wilder

With Hume Cronyn in the 1960 television version of *Juno and the Paycock*

The Sunshine Boys (1975)
with George Burns and
Richard Benjamin (right)

The Bad News Bears (1976)
with Tatum O'Neal

Casey's Shadow (1978)

House Calls (1978),
off-set with director
Howard Zieff (left)
and his son Charlie Matthau

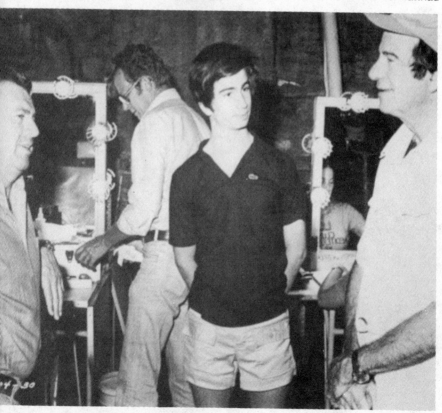

Little Miss Marker (1980) with Julie Andrews and Sara Stimson

Hopscotch (1980) with Glenda Jackson

First Monday in October (1981) with Jill Clayburgh

Chapter Ten

Always an attentive family provider Matthau had taken care not to indulge his children or encourage them to rely on living the Hollywood lifestyle for the rest of their days. His worries were the same as any other parent's – his kids' grades in school, their behaviour and what they intended to make of themselves. In the late sixties when the Matthaus were still domiciled in New York one interviewer was surprised to find them living in such an unostentatious style and even more surprised to find Matthau preoccupied with the fact that his son had gained a B in French. 'I guess my idea of rich living just doesn't happen to be having a goldplated telephone in every john. It's bad enough that Dave sees his father getting a lot of money and approval just for pulling funny faces, without my starting to act like Jean Harlow.'

One advantage of being a film actor was the time off which he could spend with Carol and his youngest son Charlie, described by his father as, 'a cross between Prince Charles and Jack Benny'. The domestic Matthau seems to like his home life to be as much fun as some of the film scripts in which he has appeared; once when he discovered Charlie and Carol in bed together he quipped: 'Don't anybody move – I'm sending for Freud!' As Charlie grew up he became his father's constant companion and even exercised his opinion on his father's choice of material. Charlie liked *The Sunshine Boys* so much that he convinced Matthau to make it his film for 1975. Around this time Matthau was considered the likeliest candidate to play W.C. Fields in the film *W.C. Fields and Me*. Rod Steiger eventually took the part.

A film version of Neil Simon's comedy *The Sunshine Boys* had been in the planning stage some time. Simon's odd couple of two feuding vaudeville veterans seemed set to provide the best roles in years for a couple of showbusiness's elder citizens. Simon even turned down a million dollar offer for the screen rights. 'Bob Hope's agent called me and offered a million dollars for the rights of *The Sunshine Boys* for Hope and Crosby. I had to wait, think about it and said no. But I couldn't get over the fact that I had turned down a million dollars! But I knew it was right. They just couldn't do that film . . .' The casting of Jack Benny and Red Skelton had almost been settled on but Skelton wasn't up to the demands of a leading role and that's where Matthau came in.

Matthau had seen the Lubitsch classic *To Be or Not to Be* with Benny and Carole Lombard on television and had an idea that he would love to do a remake with himself in the Benny role. 'A couple of days later I was having dinner with Herb Ross who started talking about *The Sunshine Boys* and said that he had just signed Jack Benny,' Matthau told reporters on the film's release. 'I asked who was in for the other role. Herb raised an eyebrow and said, "We're waiting for you".' Matthau hesitated, he had seen *The Sunshine Boys* on Broadway and considered it, 'thin, depressing and one of Neil Simon's lesser efforts'. He was to change his mind and reverse that initial impression. 'I liked the idea of working with Jack Benny but I still didn't like the script. I had another look at the script and read it across to my son Charlie – he's my constant companion and my

130

constant critic. He fell about laughing. I asked him why and he said it was because of the way I was saying the lines. Well, I've always admired his taste . . .'

Matthau and Benny began make-up tests with the latter joking about the problems involved in making them both look old enough for the roles. Benny was, in fact, seriously ill and died from cancer of the pancreas on 26 December 1974 aged eighty. Matthau was among the mourners at his memorial service three days later.

Knowing of Benny's illness the production company had asked Matthau to prepare a list of people he would accept in the Benny role if Jack became incapacitated. Top of the list was George Burns. Burns had been in semi-retirement since the death of his wife Gracie in 1964. The husband and wife team had enjoyed great popularity in radio and films of the thirties and two decades later on television. Burns hadn't appeared in a film for a very long time but, still philosophically puffing on his ever-present cigar, his timing was as fresh as ever. When his friend Benny was originally cast in the film Burns had been offered the Matthau role. Undergoing open heart surgery at the time Burns had been unable to consider the offer. Matthau didn't know him very well but admired his professionalism. 'Some twenty-five years before he had sent me a telegram offering me a regular role in his television show at $750 a week. At the time I didn't think I was worth that kind of money. The idea was so frightening I turned it down.

'He is a delightful man. He is seventy-nine but still just like a kid. He is . . . pixie-ish. Every day when you see him he makes it easier to be alive. We had a lot of fun making the film. We did not let the work get in the way too much.'

Burns was nervous about filming, after all he hadn't been on a film set in over thirty years and the studio had expressed some initial resistance to his casting. Burns need not have worried, letter-perfect and ideal in his part he could later say, 'It was the most exciting thing that ever happened to me.' *The Sunshine Boys* filmed at Metro-Goldwyn-Mayer studios in Hollywood and then departed for five weeks location-shooting in New York City including the Ansonia Hotel. Matthau had to suffer his premature ageing daily at the hands of make-up expert Dick Smith who spent over two hours adding wrinkles to his face, protruding veins to his hands and shaving his head to effect the character's baldness. The final impression, with some skilful Matthau acting thrown in, was entirely convincing to both colleagues and public. In his autobiography Burns wrote, 'When Walter arrived in the morning he had a lively bounce in his walk and he used to do little dance steps whilst he was singing or whistling; he was full of life. To show you what a complete actor Walter Matthau is, when he got up from that make-up table he not only looked like an old man, he was an old man. His whole body slumped, his shoulders sagged, his clothes hung on him, and when he walked he dragged his feet. The first day I saw him shuffle on the set I jumped up and gave him my chair. After I helped him down, he looked up and said, "Thanks, son".' On the streets of New York Matthau was approached by a lady passerby who asked, 'You are Walter Matthau aren't you?', Matthau confirmed her impression and she continued, 'They make you look much younger in the movies.'

Also in New York the duo were the subject of a testimonial dinner given by the Friars Club. During filming a warm rapport developed between Matthau and Burns, never better illustrated than in another story that Burns has recounted. 'In this one particular scene Herb thought I was playing it too serious, but he didn't say a word to me. Between takes he went to Walter and quietly told him he thought I was a little tight in this scene and asked Walter to do something to loosen me up. Well, that's all he had to say to Walter. Now, this scene was a single shot of me, and Walter was standing behind the camera feeding me lines. Herb called for action, so we started doing the scene. Right in the middle of it Walter dropped his pants. I'm sure it must have loosened me up a little, but I never lost my concentration. I went right on with the scene and, believe me, it's not easy to look a man in the eye when he's standing there with his pants down. I admit when the scene was over I did take a little peek. Walter's eyes are prettier.'

In Simon's film Willy Clark (Matthau) and Al Lewis (Burns) were one of the legendary teams from the great days of American vaudeville. The couple haven't worked together in eleven years, largely because they can't stand the sight of each other. Clark observes of Lewis, 'As an actor no one could touch him – as a human being no one wanted to.'

Lewis lives in quiet retirement with his family while Clark likes to think of himself as still active in the business, only the parts have got smaller. Willy's agent, his nephew Ben (Richard Benjamin), keeps sending him to audition for commercials and Willy keeps fouling things up with his deafness and the studied irascibility of the aged.

Ben attempts to reunite Clark and Lewis for old time's sake in a television spectacular, with disastrous consequences. All the old simmering rivalries and animosities bubble to the surface with Clark declaring, 'By the time he finishes eating, potatoes will be an endangered species.' Attempting to work on their old 'Doctor sketch' the wily Clark is so enraged that he is felled by a heart attack. Recovering in hospital it appears that the two quirky old gentlemen will play their final engagement together after all – their respective families are sending them to the same old folks' home!

Touching and funny, Simon's script is an enormously affecting piece with enough barbed humour and toughened wisecracking to cover up the genuine affection and regard between the men. Richard Benjamin, caught in the middle as the long-suffering nephew, displays a light touch and ably supports the principals. Burns is magnificent as the apparently mellower but equally malicious Al with the world's slowest circulation and a tendency to spit his words and poke Clark with his finger. Matthau, with arms rotating like an out-of-control windmill plays Willy just the right side of dementia and the part illustrates several facets of his comic talent – his ability to subtly exaggerate and seemingly over-play to great effect; and his inimitable way of delineating a character through a walk: in Willy's case with an age-worn, lead weight shuffle. With some justification Neil Simon regards *The Sunshine Boys* as the best play into film he has ever supervised. 'Oh, without doubt! I think Herb Ross is the best director I've worked with in films. The others just didn't understand my material as well. We had almost complete control with the casting, along with Ray Stark. The studio didn't want George Burns at first. Nobody thought he could act . . . He came over and read for us. Perfect!'

Matthau was worried that his performance was pitched at too unvarying a level of boorish irritability and that he had failed to find the variety in such a character. Nevertheless his teamwork with Burns is a joy to watch and the two went on an extensive tour to promote the film in America, Australia and Britain. Apart from a stop-over en route to visit the Chaplins it was his first time in Britain since the war years. 'I have been meaning to come back,' he told reporters. 'I love England. I love the English climate – the grey days, the rain . . .' He chose not to return to his old base on a sentimental pilgrimage. 'Why should I? What would I do there now? When I was there I used to come into London a lot.' In London he visited the theatre to see *No Man's Land* with John Gielgud and Ralph Richardson and said that Richardson was, 'the best actor alive. Didn't understand a word of the play. It didn't matter. It was like watching two great opera stars.'

Back in Hollywood during the spring of 1976 it was awards time. At the Golden Globes ceremony, where awards are presented by the Hollywood Foreign Press Association, *The Sunshine Boys* was named as Best Motion Picture in the musical/comedy category with Matthau Best Actor in a comedy or a musical and Richard Benjamin Best Supporting Actor. The Golden Globes make the sensible distinction between drama and comedy/musical. The Oscars make no such distinction and over the years it has proved difficult to win for comedy. One can only assume that it is necessary to suffer for one's art. At a comedy an audience is too busy enjoying itself to notice the art that provides their entertainment; in a drama they are seldom likely to forget it. At the Golden Globes ceremony Jack Nicholson had been voted a deserved Best Actor award for *One Flew Over the Cuckoo's Nest*. At the Oscar ceremony that year *Cuckoo's Nest* would sweep the board.

Matthau and Burns were both nominated for Oscars in the Best Actor and Best Supporting Actor categories respectively. Matthau faced competition from Jack Nicholson, generally considered the year's front runner, Al Pacino, nominated for *Dog Day Afternoon*, Maximilian Schell for *The Man in the Glass Booth* and James Whitmore for *Give 'em Hell, Harry*. Among Burns' fellow nominees were a strong line-up of Brad Dourif for *One Flew Over the Cuckoo's Nest*, Burgess Meredith for *The Day of the Locust*, Chris Sarandon for *Dog Day Afternoon* and Jack Warden for *Shampoo*. Playing the good sport, Matthau acted as the opening presenter in a show seen in forty-two countries. He explained the Academy's voting procedures, smoothly managed a live link-up with Amsterdam where Diana Ross was on hand to sing 'Do You Know Where You're Going To', nominated from her film *Mahogany*, and introduced the presenting couples of O. J. Simpson and Marisa Berenson, Roy Scheider and Margaux Hemingway and Madeline Kahn and Joel Grey. Matthau then handed over the proceedings to Robert Shaw.

As expected within the film business *One Flew Over the Cuckoo's Nest* was the year's major winner, taking Best Film, Best Director for Milos Forman, Best Actor for Nicholson, a surprise Best Actress for Louise Fletcher and Best Screenplay for Laurence Hauben and Bo Goldman. It was the first movie in forty-one years to sweep the board, the last such winner being *It Happened One Night* (1934). However, the most popular win of the evening came when Ben Johnson and Linda Blair stepped forward to present the Best Supporting Actor Award to George Burns. Burns, who had celebrated his eightieth birthday a few months previously, became the oldest performer ever to win an Oscar, and in his acceptance speech joked, 'This is a beautiful moment . . . Doing the picture was a great break for a newcomer like myself. The last picture I made was thirty-seven years ago and making *The Sunshine Boys* was so exciting that I'm going to make a picture every thirty-seven years.'

Matthau was delighted at his co-star's win and

philosophical about his own fate: 'I'm glad George Burns won, he deserved it. Sure I wanted to win. I still want to. I deserve it. I deserved it for *Kotch*. I've got an ego, and I play to win. I'm a gambler, both in poker and acting. Except, in acting I usually get the pay-off. I'll get another chance. If you think of awards as a tournament you're in trouble. To my mind the awards are an excellent public relations show and if you refrain from making political speeches, everything works out fine. I thought the high-pressure advertising slightly vulgar but I'm afraid you can't stop that so easily.'

By the time of the Oscar ceremony Matthau had already completed his one 1976 release, *The Bad News Bears* with a screenplay by Burt Lancaster's son Bill and a diminutive co-star in the daughter of Ryan O'Neal, Tatum. *The Bad News Bears* is a satire on the values of Middle America and a suitable companion piece to the director Michael Ritchie's earlier *Smile* (1975) which focused a similarly jaundiced eye on a Californian beauty contest. Matthau is Morris Buttermaker a beer-guzzling, over-the-hill baseball coach now reduced to cleaning swimming pools to keep body and soul together. He also coaches a team of no-hope youngsters in the junior league. The team and the coach seem to deserve each other, but when the side is joined by one outstanding player, the tomboyish Manda Whurlizer (O'Neal), it gets an injection of the competitive ethic and the team takes on a winning edge. Buttermaker realises that he is training the youngster to face the same disappointments and disillusions that he has faced so, as the team approach the little league final, he stresses the fun of playing and playing well, above the all-consuming desire for victory. In the final the Bears lose but they've all learned a lesson about self-respect and teamwork. And there's always next year.

The Bad News Bears filmed throughout the summer months of 1975 in Chatsworth, a suburb of Los Angeles where the production built a 'typical American sandlot Ballfield' and later donated it to the area. The children had been cast from a nationwide search, centring on Los Angeles, Texas and New York. Tatum O'Neal had been specially coached by her father to get by in the pitching scenes. Producer Stanley Jaffe recalled, 'We filmed in the hottest part of the valley, it was something like 107 in the shade, the kids' feet were burning up on the playing field. Walter just had to keep out of the sun because of his heart condition but he would never go into his camper but stayed around, fooling with the kids and telling stories. He was like a Pied Piper during the filming. One little Mexican boy said that he'd passed Walter's house at the weekend. Walter asked him why he hadn't dropped in and the kid said something like he didn't feel it was right. So, Walter had the kid, and his family, and his friends up to his house. He's a wonderful, lovely man.'

Matthau's role in *The Bad News Bears* was ideal because he had, after all, been a sports coach and his wry, shop-soiled screen persona was well-suited to a disenchanted old cuss with a heart of gold. The bad-temperedness of previous screen characterisations was slipping to let show a tender compassion beneath the gruff exterior; on screen he was becoming lovable. In a number of family films towards the end of the decade he seemed to be exchanging the mantle of W.C. Fields for that of someone more akin to Wallace Beery. Fields admitted to liking children well-boiled, but Matthau worked well with Tatum O'Neal and expressed his admiration for her: 'Imagine the kid got an Academy Award at the age of nine; it is easy to work with her but you must not forget that her father, Ryan O'Neal, is a

star and star kids live under abnormal circumstances.'
As to Peter Bogdanovich's description of her as 'Ten,
going on thirty-five', Matthau responded, 'Tatum is ten
going on eleven. The trouble is that people treat her as
ten going on thirty-five. She's just a little girl. She's
delightful if you treat her as a little girl, but if you treat
her as a lady it can be very sticky.'

The Bad News Bears works well on two levels; both as a
fresh, funny comedy and as a film with something to say
about the values of life, with the Little League Bears a
microcosm for a wider society. It was also a smash hit,
the number four film in the list of top money-makers
released in America during 1976.

Tatum O'Neal had been paid $350,000 for her part in
The Bad News Bears, allegedly the highest-ever
remuneration given a child performer. Matthau received
$750,000 against ten per cent of the first eight million
dollars of gross receipts, twelve to twelve and a half per
cent of the next five million dollars and fifteen per cent of
everything over thirteen million dollars. These involved
arrangements became public knowledge when Matthau
sued Paramount several years later. His film had been
such a huge success that the company had quickly
produced two sequels – The Bad News Bears in Breaking
Training (1977) with William Devane and The Bad News
Bears Go To Japan (1978) with Tony Curtis. In 1978
Paramount sold the films for television screening in
America to ABC for eighteen and a half million dollars
and allocated roughly similar amounts to the balance
sheets of the three films. Matthau objected to this
believing that his original film had been by far the
biggest money-spinner, and thus brought his suit in the
Los Angeles Superior Court in the early months of 1979.
It was believed that The Bad News Bears had grossed
almost thirty-five million dollars within the United

States and this was, 'primarily attributable to Matthau's stature as a box-office attraction and his widely acclaimed performance'. The second 'Bears' film grossed around $14,500,000 and the third almost $6,500,000 illustrating, if nothing else, the law of diminishing returns. The suit, in essence, claimed that Paramount had unfairly distributed the proceeds of the television sale among the individual films after having used Matthau's star value to sell the package in the first place, thus depriving the star of his profit participation.

Paramount had allocated six million, seven hundred and fifty thousand dollars to 'Bears 1', six million, two hundred and fifty thousand to 'Bears 2' and five and a half million to 'Bears 3'. Matthau claimed that his film alone would have been worth twelve million dollars if sold to the networks, which was some five million, two hundred and fifty thousand dollars less than Paramount would rate it. Using the arithmetic of fifteen per cent of that figure Matthau had personally lost out on $787,500. In his suit he demanded that money plus a million dollars punitive damages for 'willful breach of fiduciary dues'.

On the surface, for a wealthy film star to go through a long, involved legal procedure to recoup even more money from a film that had already rewarded him well seems a little excessive. However, when that star comes from a cripplingly poor background and he happens to be in the right, then hell hath no greater fury than a poor New Yorker cheated out of what is rightly his. Hollywood was involved in several cases where profit-participation schemes proved less than fruitful through skilful accounting procedures and Matthau wasn't about to be duped.

Matthau had endured the fierce sun-baked locations for *The Bad News Bears* with equanimity. Since his heart attack some ten years before he had moved to a healthier climate, was now a financial success without the frenzied highs and lows of a gambler's life, and had followed an exercise regime of daily, long brisk walks. However in April 1976 he entered the Daniel Freeman hospital in Inglewood for a four-hour heart by-pass operation. A medical check-up had discovered the abnormality and the doctors decided to carry out surgery. A spokesman said, 'Walter was advised to have surgery to prevent a possible heart attack which would have proved fatal in future years. It wasn't immediately necessary.'

Matthau explained: 'After my heart attack I went on a programme of walking every day. I walked four of five miles at one time at a rather rapid pace. I did that every day. I've been feeling fine ever since. No trouble. Just a little angina in the middle of a four-mile walk uphill one day and I went in for a coronary angiogram. It showed a definite occlusion in the left anterior descending.

'I knew that that's the artery that can't be clogged so I said, "How soon can you do it?" They said, "Tomorrow morning". I really didn't even have time to be scared.'

Scared or not, Matthau, characteristically, handled the situation with a joke: 'One doctor told me to take it easy and get plenty of rest, the other said I needed to exercise more so I did press-ups in bed.'

The press-ups must have helped for he was back at work within a few months. In August he began filming *Casey's Shadow* under director Martin Ritt. The production of this film became a long, protracted affair. The first sequences, shot in August, contained the climax of the picture. After a break the production was completed in December with the filming of a colt's birth and the technicians were busy readying everything for a release at Easter 1977. But by April 1977 Ritt had decided that the ending of the film was all wrong in terms of what had gone before and was granted the hard-won right to shoot a different ending, delaying the film's release until 1978. The film's producer, Ray Stark, had taken some persuasion before coming round to Ritt's point of view. 'I told him I was no young director, that he wasn't going to stop me or I'd take a friggin' advertisement out in every paper in the United States, would never work for him again . . . in addition to which I'd kick in a few windows,' Ritt claims. 'I just didn't want a sentimental ending, but something more amusing, saying something about the nature of the family involved. And that's what I did. I'd never had the luxury of re-shooting before and they didn't squawk too much in the end.'

In *Casey's Shadow*, decked out with a luxurious moustache and a bogus Cajun accent, Matthau plays Lloyd Bourdell a ne'er-do-well horse trainer who has to raise three sons on his own when his wife leaves him.

By a stroke of luck he picks up a lightning-fast young horse and feels that he has a chance of training a winner for the All-Americas Race. So confident is he of victory that he spares no one, including his children and the well-being of the horse. Against even his own best principles he runs the horse in the final of the All Americas race and wins. However, the horse is lame and will have to be put down. His children have lost the blind faith they had in their father and go to work for wealthy ranch-owner Sarah Blue (Alexis Smith) who had made a bid of half a million dollars for the horse when it was in sound condition.

Lloyd, however, redeems himself. He explains that he was consumed by the one last chance to show his worth and be somebody by having his name in the record books. He pays all the prize money to a vet to give 'Casey's Shadow' a chance for the bones to mend, and the horse survives. The family, once again low on finances, is reunited – all working for Sarah Blue.

Casey's Shadow is light family fare with some substance to it, some interesting locales, a salty line or two of dialogue and accomplished performances. Matthau definitely finds himself in Wallace Beery territory with this one but it is a mark of his true star quality that he carries the proceedings along in an engaging manner, adding charm and weight to his lynchpin performance as the beer-guzzling, loving paterfamilias. The reappearance of Alexis Smith was more than welcome and Robert Webber, as a smarmy rival, had some of the best lines. Unable to believe in Lloyd's good fortune he trumpets, 'You haven't had your hands on anything with speed since your wife ran off' and adds that of the last two horses Lloyd was enthusiastic over 'neither one could beat my dog with a full bladder'. *Casey's Shadow* was perhaps a mite too leisurely and amiable because it turned out to be a box-office flop. The family audience that turned out in droves to see *The Black Stallion* in 1979 stayed away in similar numbers from *Casey's Shadow*. Ritt, whose usual forte is films with a social conscience, was used to public resistance to films with a message but felt that *Casey's Shadow* would be different. 'When I'd finished it, I told my wife, "We're really going to get rich. I've finally made a film that is not going to offend any segment of the audience!" Everybody loved it and I got, all in all, probably as good reviews as I've ever gotten on a film, even though it was a light film. I mean, I never thought it was any great shakes. Just very entertaining. Well . . . nobody went to see it. I never understood it.'

The long delays on *Casey's Shadow* produced a log-jam in the release of Matthau's films and he ended up with three pictures on display in 1978, a year which found him at number thirteen in the top twenty box-office stars' list. The other two releases were *House Calls*, a memorable first encounter with double Oscar-winner Glenda Jackson, and *California Suite*, a disappointingly flat reunion with Neil Simon and Herbert Ross.

House Calls, filmed during the British school holidays, allowed Jackson to fly over to Hollywood with her son Daniel for her first American film and enjoy something akin to a holiday with pay. Jackson made the trip for one strong reason: 'Walter Matthau! It was the opportunity of working with him. I couldn't pass that up. He's wonderful and it's so marvellous to work with someone like that. That's why I came. And also it's a good, funny script, although the character I play is a bit fleshless.'

In 1978 the brash, unsubtle *National Lampoon's Animal House*, starring John Belushi, became the highest-grossing film comedy ever. In an era when sophistication meant Belushi removing the food from his mouth before speaking, *House Calls* was a welcome contrast. The film impresses as a romantic, adult comedy with a touch of class. Matthau found, 'the texture very inviting, and the words very attractive and since I've been hanging around with doctors for the last twenty-five years I thought it would be nice to play a doctor now and do anything that I wanted to do. It seems to me that doctors do anything they want and behave any way and quite often don't know what they're doing.'

Dr Charley Nichols (Matthau) was a happily married and faithful husband. Now a widower, he decides to make up for lost time and play the field, until he meets his match in Ann Atkinson (Jackson) an English divorcée with a son, Michael (Charlie Matthau). The couple agree to two weeks' fidelity before facing the possibility of marriage. Misunderstandings abound and tempers flare. At one point Atkinson, a receptionist at the hospital where Nichols works, hides his clothes whilst he's in the shower and he has to turn up to work in drag. Eventually the couple make it back together again.

A lot of the fun in *House Calls* comes from the maladministration of the hospital where Nichols is embroiled with colleagues Dr Norman Solomon (Richard Benjamin) and the dangerously senile and incompetent Dr Amos Willoughby (Art Carney). Matthau, as the crumpled medic who hasn't had a real date since 1948, and Jackson as a woman with a mind of her own, make a pleasing combination. The director Howard Zieff admired their teamwork, commenting during filming, 'The chemistry between Glenda and Walter is just marvellous. They look wonderful together. If we're lucky, it's true that this could turn out to be a special kind of romantic comedy like Tracy and Hepburn used to make.' The film went on to gross some fifteen million dollars and spawned a hit television series.

Matthau, occasionally accident-prone during filming, found *House Calls* one of those occasions when he was involved in a slight accident. 'I was rehearsing a scene with Glenda in which we were lying in bed watching an old Joan Crawford movie. And in that movie there's a scene of Crawford kissing her leading man and then the camera turns to the windows which are open with the curtains blowing. It's a sure sign that some amorous lovemaking is going on behind the scenes.

'Then Glenda tells me that in those days you weren't allowed to show a man and a woman in bed unless they were on opposite sides of the bed and each one had a foot on the floor. I say that making love is impossible with one foot on the floor and on opposite sides of the bed and then we go into a series of contortions, when I'm sort of bent up like a pretzel, we fell off the bed! I thought I'd broken my foot but it turned out just to be sprained. It was quite painful I can tell you!' Despite his minor injuries Matthau had nothing but praise for the film and his leading lady, 'She's an absolute dreamboat who is the epitome of professionalism. She's a splendid actress and has all the make-up of a fully rounded person.'

Matthau's final 1978 release, which appeared in America for Christmas and was chosen as the 1979 Royal Film Performance in Britain, was Neil Simon's *California Suite*. A reunion with Simon and director Herbert Ross, with Elaine May playing his wife, must have appeared rather attractive. However, the Matthau-May sketch is not the best material in Simon's four-tiered comic extravaganza. Far better were Maggie Smith and Michael Caine as a bickering showbusiness couple and Jane Fonda and Alan Alda fighting over the custody of their child.

Matthau plays Marvin Michaels who is in Los Angeles for his nephew's barmitzvah. He arrives one day before his wife Millie (May) and spends the evening on the town with his brother, who has arranged for him to have the company of an attractive blonde for the evening. The following morning the blonde, in a drunken stupor, is in bed with Marvin when his wife arrives at the hotel. Marvin frantically tries to conceal the unwanted female but Millie discovers his secret. Unexpectedly she proves wise and forgiving. This third segment of the Simon screenplay was a rather tired, formula skit to which Matthau and May can add little. However, Matthau admitted, 'When I was making *California Suite* Herbert Ross kept after me, saying, "You're not trying; you're not trying." He was really rough on me. But he was right.'

Chapter Eleven

Approaching sixty – and getting there faster according to independent estimates than by his own – Matthau was publicly expressing his disenchantment with the double-edged sword that is fame. The acclaim he received for *The Odd Couple* and *The Fortune Cookie* brought a career rich in success, both financial and creative, public recognition and a batting average of hits as high as any in Hollywood. But running alongside this were the drawbacks; a star is firmly placed within a certain frame of reference and has a specific image attached to his success, an image that is generally a very hard one to escape from. 'I've developed a definite character,' he explained in an 1980 interview, 'and I have to pay the price. I can't play any dramatic roles, let alone the great ones anymore, yet I would like to. People are always sending me domestic comedies which they say they wrote specially for me. I read one or two pages, then throw them out. Mind you, I'd play a man with gonorrhea who walks around with different coloured shoes if the auspices were good. Producers come to me and say, "Sure you're our number one choice. Steve, Robert, Marlon turned it down . . ." But you can't get away from the hierarchy. If I do a million-dollar picture, then accept $75,000 for the next one, I'm a $75,000 actor. That's Hollywood for you.'

As a relatively unknown performer Matthau had been asked to essay an outrageous Hungarian film-producer, a laconic sheriff, Runyonesque heavies and gangsters, Western baddies and best friends, Sean O'Casey one moment and a leering neighbourhood wolf the next. That range and diversity of casting seemed lost to him after he became a star. With several notable exceptions he has played almost exclusively within the perimeters of domestic comedy since 1966. It is a genre for which he has a monumental talent but such a monotonous diet is bound to provoke a rebellion. In theory stardom meant being bankable and using that clout to finance the 'dirty poem' or whatever he might find interesting. In practice that was rarely the case. 'Hollywood is a company town,' he said in the same interview. 'We're all working for Big Brother. We're peons and serfs allowed to work here by the good graces of the master of the territory. I'm not an independent spirit. That's a lot of shit. I do what I have to do. I may be the highest priced serf in the business but I'm still a serf. I'm a whore, no question.'

His rather jaundiced view of stardom can't have been helped by an incident during the summer of 1978. Matthau received a letter demanding one hundred and fifty thousand dollars or his son Charlie, then fifteen, would meet 'great bodily harm'. Matthau alerted the police and telephone instructions were followed by leaving a suitcase full of money in a designated spot. When a youth moved in to collect the money he was arrested. Eighteen-year-old Kenneth Dahlinger was charged with extortion. It was an illustration of another drawback of stardom: that you become a moving target for every crank and criminal.

It is a mark of the complexity of Matthau that, despite the grumbles, he still took pride in his profession and wasn't too churlish to enjoy the late arrival of his star status and the accompanying comforts. Both his sons have entered their father's business and Matthau has been on hand to lend a guiding hand. David graduated from the University of Southern California, majoring in cinema, his other subjects being speech and drama. He had been under contract to Universal Studios, appearing in several of their television series including *The Love Boat*, *The Bionic Woman* and *Operation Petticoat*. In films he had gained small parts in *FM*, *The Big Fix* and *Battlestar Galactica* (all 1978 releases) and *Airport '79-the Concorde*. He had also turned up in several Neil Simon comedies: *The Goodbye Girl* (1977), *The Cheap Detective* (1978) and *California Suite* (1978). In the latter film he played a hotel bellboy in his father's segment of the screenplay. Charlie had appeared in *Charley Varrick* (1973) and *House Calls* (1978) before moving over to the other side of the camera. In subsequent years he would become involved in the production side of his father's work usually in the capacity of associate producer. Matthau's stepdaughter Lucy Saroyan has also worked in the film world, appearing in the Richard Pryor films *Greased Lightning* (1978) and *Blue Collar* (1978).

The jaundiced, high-priced 'serf' probably revealed his true colours when questioned as to his feelings about having a family following in his footsteps, 'I think the whole business of being an actor and being part of entertainment, whether it be TV shows or stage shows or movies, is noble,' he said. 'You learn about everything and you're involved in something. You know what it is – it's acting. Look at the doctors and the lawyers. They think they're real people.'

In 1979 he began work on a long-cherished project – a remake of *Little Miss Marker*. A classic Damon Runyon tale of a sour bookie saddled with a winsome young miss, the story had first seen the light of day in 1934 with

Adolphe Menjou and Shirley Temple taking the lead roles. Over the years it had been refashioned into a successful vehicle for the talents of Bob Hope in *Sorrowful Jones* (1949) and Tony Curtis in *40 Pounds of Trouble* (1963). Matthau had regarded the role of 'Sorrowful Jones' as tailor-made and had considered the film as a project for virtually two decades. He was so convinced by the worth of the idea that he displayed his commitment by handling the job of executive producer. In seeking a screenplay writer he approached Walter Bernstein. They had first met during the filming of *Fail Safe*. Bernstein, with many notable screen credits, including *The Train* (1964) and *The Front* (1976), had often worked with Matthau's friend Martin Ritt and agreed to write the script if Matthau would allow him to direct as well. Matthau had long admired Bernstein as one of the best screenwriters in the world and accepted his terms declaring, 'If anyone can improve on Damon Runyon, it's Walter Bernstein. Sorrowful Jones was made to order for me. This is classic sceptical, hard-bitten experience versus love and innocence, and how love and innocence wins.'

Matthau then began to assemble around him a highly experienced cast of comic performers and former co-stars including Lee Grant from *Plaza Suite*, Tony Curtis from *Goodbye Charlie* and Bob Newhart. His leading lady, for the first time, was Julie Andrews, making one of her irregular film appearances and the first in over a decade which was not in a film directed by her husband Blake Edwards. Her reasons for accepting the part were: 'The screenplay and Walter Matthau. The chance of working with him is so lovely and the screenplay by Walter Bernstein is really charming.'

The ingratiating moppet, played to perfection by little Shirley Temple almost fifty years before, was portrayed by the equally diminutive Sara Stimson, a co-star of disarming honesty, as Matthau discovered. 'This little kid Sara Stimson she tells it the way it is. Once when I picked her up and kissed her she said: "Ugh – your breath smells." So I had to rush off and buy some strong mouthwash. Another time she stuck her finger in my face. "Don't do that," I said, "You will make a crease." "What's a crease?" she demanded. "A wrinkle," I said. "But you've got a lot of those already," she said. Charming kid.'

Filming proceeded in diverse Californian locations, including the Los Angeles County Museum of Natural History, the Long Beach amusement park, the Sonoma County Fairgrounds and Wilmington Pier. Matthau expressed his unease with his extra functions on the film: 'I'm a producer in name only. I hate power. I despise the fact that I have any say at all in what is going on. But I'm happy to be working. Working is so much easier than not working. And Walter Bernstein is a good director. He is a first-rate talent with a first rate mind. Now me, I'm a first rate talent with a fourth rate mind. At least I assume I'm a first rate talent since they're paying me all this money. Otherwise I wouldn't be so cocky. It's the self-loathing syndrome.' On the surface Matthau was becoming tinsel town's master of self-deprecation, ever-ready to put himself down with a wisecrack or a witty *bon mot*. How seriously one should take such comments is debatable. One self-defence mechanism for the shy is to belittle their abilities before anyone else does. Yet Matthau was now so well-established that any self-doubts or self-critical analysis seem an excessive indulgence. His talent is unquestionable, yet his oft-voiced sentiments of self-doubt reveal one of the many complexities in his seemingly easy-going, laugh-a-minute personality.

151

Little Miss Marker's failure at the box-office was a curious event. A wholesome family comedy, even old-fashioned and sentimental, it seemed ideal for a year in which the mood of the American nation was one of looking over their shoulder to re-establish the values of another era. With innocence and goodness triumphant over the mean and petty it would have appeared the perfect fare for a people voting Ronald Reagan president. Instead the film was criticised as old hat, slowly paced and dull. Julie Andrews was out of place, Sara Stimson wasn't Shirley Temple and everyone was awaiting the pyrotechnics of *The Empire Strikes Back*. In Britain the critics were kinder; the review in the magazine *Films Illustrated* stated: 'let us enjoy it for its craftsmanship and its sound performances. Matthau has seldom been better: though writer Walter Bernstein (here directing for the first time) was evidently inviting him to overplay, it is a temptation the actor largely resists.' It was some consolation, but the ticket-buying public still stayed away. Disappointed, Matthau's only comment was, 'It was too intellectual for the critics and audiences.'

Soon after finishing work on *Little Miss Marker*, Matthau welcomed a chance to work again with Glenda Jackson. He readily agreed to make *Hopscotch*, despite the very short break between films. As he said, working was easier than doing nothing.

Hopscotch, a light spy thriller, had once been announced as a project for Michael Caine and Jane Fonda and, in June 1977, Cliff Robertson had apparently consented to appear in it. Eventually Matthau wound up top dog in a production based on the novel by Arizona-born Brian Garfield, a former Western pulp magazine writer. *Hopscotch* had been the recipient of the Mystery Writers of America's Edgar Award as the Best

Novel of 1975. Filming seemed likely to be a globe-trotting affair but Matthau was undaunted by the rigours of the schedule. 'When I first met the film's producers, Edie and Ely Landau, and author Brian Garfield, we chatted about this and that for a while. Then they asked me how I felt about an eleven-week schedule that included a car chase, an airplane chase and plenty of other action scenes on locations in Germany, Austria, England and the United States. I said I had once suffered a heart attack and I told them, "My doctor gave me six months to live, and then when I couldn't pay the bill, he gave me six months more." They all laughed and looked relieved, so I accepted the part.'

With globe-scattered locations in Salzburg, Marseilles, Bermuda, London, Savannah in Atlanta and Washington DC the eight million-dollar production of *Hopscotch* began filming in Munich during the city's famous Oktoberfest. Surrounded by a leading lady he admired, a strong supporting cast that included his son David, and a ready audience for his wisecracks and anecdotes Matthau gained obvious enjoyment from his time on the film. He celebrated his birthday in Salzburg, sharing a glass of wine with Glenda Jackson for their first scenes together in the Winkler Cafe and Casino. After work the cast and crew celebrated at the Schloss Fuchsel and the film's director Ronald Neame gave Matthau a birthday present of an eighteenth-century duelling pistol.

The Matthau-Jackson mutual appreciation society continued to flourish and their comments illustrate a genuine professional respect that is rare and untarnished by any false Hollywood baloney. Matthau enthused, 'Glenda is great. She's so easy to work with, intelligent, always knows her lines and we hit it off well as a team. You can't ask anything more of your leading lady. She's a number one talent and terrific lady. I've worked with every sort of big name actress you could mention. Half of them are pains in the ass. Some are just plain stupid. One actress-singer thought she was God's gift to directors – I had to tell her to do her job and let the director direct. Another one has this real liberal image, and said after three dramatic pictures she was glad to have the chance to "relax" in a Neil Simon comedy – I told her she'd probably bore the audience out of their pants.

'But Glenda is class and she's fun. I love working with her. I'd love to work with her again. I could say that about anybody, but the proof is that we do work together repeatedly.' The fact that Jackson was willing to accept a subsidiary role, and an even more 'fleshless' one than her part in *House Calls*, just to work with Matthau again, speaks volumes for the regard in which she holds the actor.

The director Ronald Neame also voiced a high regard for the two stars. Neame's career stretched back to Alfred Hitchcock's *Blackmail* (1929), the first British 'talkie', on which Neame had acted as assistant-cameraman. A distinguished cinematographer he had turned to direction in 1947 working, over the years, with some of the industry's best actors including Alec Guinness, Judy Garland, Robert Mitchum and Sean Connery. For someone who might be expected to have attuned himself to the star quality of top performers Neame was enraptured by the Matthau-Jackson chemistry. 'How long the camera stays on a performer's face after he or she has delivered a line of dialogue is a good indication of how good that actor is,' Neame explained. 'With the average actor, the natural tendency is to cut away from the close-up on the face to something else after a line is read. With truly outstanding performers, such as Walter and Glenda, I have to be careful not to stay on the face too long. The temptation is there, because a really good actor can often say more with his face than an ordinary actor can with ten lines of dialogue.'

Matthau appears to like his film sets professionally run but casual and fun. *Hopscotch* was no exception and, playing it resolutely deadpan, he told one visiting journalist, 'I'm inclined to believe that there's much similarity between a secret agent and an actor. In both jobs there are times when you have to rely on your wits, your initiative and your skills. And, in return, you enjoy recognition, positions of responsibility, life in foreign places, plus the satisfaction of knowing that you belong to a small but very special group of people doing a vital, meaningful task in the face of challenges and maybe even possible hardship.

'To me, that sounds just like a movie actor on location.'

Little Miss Marker opened in America in March 1980 and in Britain around six months later. It was not a success. The Damon Runyon story finds Matthau as Sorrowful Jones, a miserly bookie who makes Scrooge look positively philanthropic. An unlucky gambler has persuaded Sorrowful to give him credit for a ten dollar bet, leaving his young daughter as a marker. The man commits suicide leaving 'the Kid' an orphan and Sorrowful with a problem. And it's not the only one – mobster Blackie Ryan (Tony Curtis) is after Sorrowful to invest $50,000 in a gambling house and is going to make him an offer he won't refuse. Sorrowful pays Blackie the money and inspects the casino which is run by Amanda (Julie Andrews), a socialite who has fallen on hard times.

Sorrowful, Amanda and 'the Kid' become an inseparable trio, taking a keen interest in Amanda's racehorse Sir Galahad. When the casino goes bust Blackie decides to recoup his losses by doping the horse and fixing a race. Sorrowful acts to save Amanda's horse, put Blackie out of the picture and secure a future for 'the Kid' to whom he has become grudgingly attached. When the only solution seems to be the marriage of Sorrowful and Amanda, Sorrowful displays all the characteristics of a caring human being and proposes, thus ensuring an all-round happy ending.

Hopscotch was released six months after *Little Miss Marker* and proved a resounding hit. Attractively photographed, *Hopscotch* found Matthau in his element as CIA agent Miles Kendig, a loyal company man who has always played by his own rules. He successfully breaks up a spy ring in Munich but allows his eminently civilised adversary Mikhail Yaskow (Herbert Lom) to go free. The latter action so enrages his newly-promoted chief Myerson (Ned Beatty) that Kendig is given a desk job and his assistant Cutter (Sam Waterson) is given his position. Kendig quits, shreds his personal file and heads for Salzburg and a reunion with Isobel von Schmidt (Glenda Jackson), a beautiful widow, formerly an employee of the agency. From then on Kendig and Isobel lead the spy agencies of the world on a merry chase. Kendig writes an exposé of international espionage, sending a chapter at a time to his pursuers. Eventually, having staged his own death, Kendig lives to enjoy the fruits of his revenge having outwitted his colleagues once again.

Hopscotch is Matthau's show all the way. Jackson's Isobel is little more than a cipher to aid the plot and develop the romantic interest and while the secondary roles are filled by a strong calibre of performer, they are still very much secondary roles. The film itself is a light, polished, civilised entertainment. *Time* magazine hit the nail on the head with the comment, 'He (Matthau) does what a star must do: he creates the illusion that this film is better than it actually is.'

1980 was largely a year of reflection and inactivity on the film front. Of the two Matthau films released there was a fifty per cent success rate and Matthau was twelfth among the top box-office stars that year. During the year he had been scheduled to begin a new film, *Thanks Dad*, an examination of a father-son relationship to be directed by Walter Bernstein. The film was a casualty of the actors' strike of that summer which closed down production throughout Hollywood. Another casualty of the strike appears to have been the projected co-starring of Matthau with Al Pacino in a film entitled *Tubie's Monument*. He was offered the role of Philo Skinner, a sleazy dog-handler, in *The Black Marble* adapted from the Joseph Wambaugh novel. However, he was more interested in the leading role of Sgt Valnikov which was already taken by Robert Foxworth and thus decided not to make the film.

The actors' strike was largely initiated by uncertainty over the repercussions of the lightning advances in technology that were beginning to make their presence felt in the entertainment industry. Video and cable are the bread and butter for future generations of performers and members of the industry wanted to know just where they stood as regards payment. The strike concerned actors' royalties from Pay TV and video and cable rights to their work. The producers wanted too much of the pie for themselves. Matthau rallied to the defence of his fellow workers and volunteered for picket duty; it was a way of declaring his empathy with the less fortunate in the profession he admires so much. He also used his star status to publicise the actors' demands – among them a new minimum wage of $340 a day, a rise of some $100.

To the big-earning stars such figures were irrelevant,

but after picket duty outside Warner Brothers studios he told a reporter, 'Some actors only get a couple of jobs a year. If we get what we are asking for, they might just be able to earn a decent living.' Emphasising the future development of the new technology he pointed out, 'I know it sounds outrageous but within a decade it is likely that everyone will be getting their entertainment entirely at home by simply turning a knob.' And as if to blur the concern and care he had shown he made light of his own involvement, making sure to mention the camaraderie ('I had a marvellous time. I must have seen at least forty people I didn't know were still alive.') and the girls ('There they were walking up and down in their tight shorts with their breasts bursting to spill out of their tops. Tremendous!').

Less tremendous was a misunderstanding with the Screen Actors' Guild which ordered him to appear before its trial committee to face a charge of 'conduct unbecoming a member' for which he could have been fined, suspended or expelled. One Friday during the eighth week of the strike Matthau had been present for a press conference with twenty-five journalists to promote the film *Hopscotch* for producer Ely Landau. This appeared to be in direct breach of a Guild ban on all promotion work. However, as a non-studio producer Landau had signed an independent agreement with the Guild and Matthau was therefore in the clear as the ban didn't apply in the *Hopscotch* case. The Guild dropped the order and subsequently apologised to Matthau.

Throughout the year Matthau continued to reveal the pitfalls of stardom and the difficulty of knowing what to do next. 'An agent recently called me and asked whether I'd like to go to London to play in *Uncle Vanya* with Glenda. I'd love to go, but I know I wouldn't be acceptable to English audiences. And they'd be quite right,' he told one interviewer. A man who bemoans that he can never play the classics again but turns down a chance to do *Uncle Vanya* just has to be a figure fraught with contradictions.

Judging by some public pronouncements there was certainly a part of him that felt hemmed in. 'I just spoke to my agent. I told him I wanted to do something in an eight-hour TV special they're going to make in Israel. He was shocked, "You can't do TV," he said. "That's not good for your career." Isn't that depressing? I've elevated myself to a position where I can no longer do the things I want to do. It's as if someone said: "You're too fine, too noble to have sex. You're the King. Girls are out!"' Yet, one would imagine that the remedy was in his own hands and that a well-established star on the eve of his sixtieth birthday needn't have too many worries about what might affect his career. If the Hollywood money men wouldn't finance a risky project then there was always the stage. Matthau had an answer to that as well. 'A while ago, Neil Simon wrote a play for me called *I Ought to Be in Pictures* which is currently on Broadway. He rang me up when he had finished writing it and told me all about it.

'In the next breath he said he didn't think I should do it. "Why not?", I asked. "Well," said Neil, "it would mean you'd have to leave sunny California, spend time away from your family, work six days a week for maybe a year, and, on top of that, have to cope with New York, which can be dirty, dangerous and downright unpleasant."

'None the less, I said, I still wanted to read the play. "Okay," said Neil, and he sent the script round. The following day I called him and told him I loved the play but that I wasn't going to do it. "Why not?" he asked.

' "Well," I said, "it would mean I'd have to leave sunny

California, spend time away from my family, work six days a week for maybe a year, and, on top of that, have to put up with New York which can be dirty, dangerous and downright unpleasant."

'The fact is, the older I get the easier I want to take things. And working in a Broadway play is much, much harder work than making a movie. Despite the money we all make in Hollywood, being a movie actor is like being semi-employed.

'And, frankly, at this stage in my life, that's just the way I like it.'

Thus, to balance the part of him which feels restricted, there is another part which acknowledges his age and the benefits of a California lifestyle and reckons that the life of a movie-star isn't half bad. He seems to have accepted the contradictions in his own character when he states: 'I have been lucky. Perhaps because for all my crying about artistic merit I do have a crass commercial streak. For that reason if they offered me Macbeth I'd probably turn it down on the grounds that it's not commercial. Also on the grounds that perhaps I can't play Macbeth. Nothing is easy. I'm insecure and I thrive on it. I love living on the brink. Anyway I'm not at all sure that security is a good thing. Otherwise why are these people in Sweden always committing suicide.'

With the actors' strike resolved he chose to film the well-heeled stage play *The First Monday In October* by Jerome Lawrence and Robert E. Lee about the appointment of the first woman to the Supreme Court. The first production had been in October 1975 as part of the sixtieth anniversary celebrations of the Cleveland Playhouse and had starred Melvyn Douglas and Jean Arthur. After rewrites the play opened at the Kennedy Centre in Washington on 26 December 1977 with Henry Fonda and Jane Alexander, eventually travelling to

Broadway the following year and touring in Los Angeles and Chicago where Eva Marie Saint replaced Jane Alexander. When it came to the film version ill-health prevented Fonda recreating his role and a star teaming of William Holden and Ellen Burstyh was announced. Holden is believed to have been very enthusiastic about the film but, in a casting turn-around characteristic of the musical chairs that often transpires between initiation and realisation, Matthau wound up playing opposite Jill Clayburgh.

The title of the piece derives from the first meeting of the High Court every autumn to resume business after the summer recess. Given the crucial placing of the film at a specific time of year, the production was locked into filming over a limited time. Delayed by the strike, filming began on 21 October in Washington where the pressure was on to complete production before the onset of winter. Chief Justice Warren Burger had seen the Fonda-Alexander play and helped the film company to gain permission to shoot on the steps of the Supreme Court Building. Permission was granted to film only on the steps and only on a Saturday when the Court was not in session. The interior scenes were completed on a half-million dollar set built on the Paramount lot back in Hollywood. Other scenes took place at the Smithsonian Institute and the Arlington National cemetery where the funeral of a Supreme Court Justice was filmed with Matthau giving the eulogy. 'I've never performed a scene in more distinguished company,' Matthau said. 'We filmed it next to the graves of Oliver Wendell Holmes and William O. Douglas while the J.F.K. grave was just over the knoll.'

With President Reagan's appointment of Sandra Day O'Connor to the Supreme Court, *First Monday in October* gained a certain unexpected topicality and the film's release was brought forward by several months.

The events that unfold in *The First Monday in October* are triggered by the death of one of the nine Justices of the Supreme Court. The replacement is a widow, Ruth Loomis (Jill Clayburgh), an arch-conservative and the first woman ever to be appointed. Judge Dan Snow (Matthau) welcomes the choice of a woman but not one with her politics. The two first clash over the case of an allegedly pornographic film *The Naked Nymphomaniac*. Regardless of her politics Loomis believes it is her duty to view the entire film. However distasteful the experience she has to see every minute before a valid judgement can be made. Snow believes that adults have the right to see anything and does not even attend the screening.

In a debate Loomis argues that the nation's youth must be protected, Snow counter-argues the need for liberty and freedom from censorship. Diametrically opposed on their political stance towards most issues, the couple grow to respect each other's intelligence and ability. When Snow's wife leaves him the couple see more of each other and become engrossed in a case about a multinational corporation. When Snow is hospitalised with a heart attack Loomis continues her investigations and uncovers the unpleasant fact that through her late husband's law firm she has been involved in a cover up. Feeling morally bound to resign she is only persuaded not to by Snow who has left his hospital bed to convince her of the need to stay. The two return to court together.

A literate, often academic film, the appeal of *The First Monday in October* was limited by sticking too closely to its stage origins and by a lack of dramatic punch, but enhanced by the elegant teamwork of Matthau and Clayburgh. The critical consensus was favourably inclined towards the performers but felt it was a film for the older generation – a generation that didn't go to the movies that often any more. Matthau was disgruntled by this limitation placed on his appeal and said so. 'I've read one review for my new film. It said that the commercial prospects seemed bright – "particularly with those middle-aged filmgoers who frequently emerge for Matthau". My agent, who is a first class idiot, made it even worse. He went one step further than the imbecile who wrote the review. Before I'd seen it he called and told me it said I brought out the "elderly" people – as if I dragged them out like worms from under a stone. The fact is my biggest audience could well be between eleven and fourteen. After all they're the ones who turned out to see me in *The Bad News Bears*.'

The First Monday in October had completed filming in January 1981 and within a month the normally cautious Matthau was back at work on another film, *Buddy, Buddy*. The reason was self-evident: 'I never say no to Billy Wilder. As a matter of fact I would have signed up to star for Billy Wilder with Jack Lemmon without reading a script. Wilder's my favourite director.'

Buddy, Buddy was not a project which Wilder initiated. The production partnership of Jay Weston and Alain Bernheim had acquired rights to a French farce, *L'Emmerdeur* which had been released abroad as *A Pain in the A****. The French production had come to the screen under the aegis of the future *Cage aux Folles* team of director Edouard Molinaro and writer Francis Veber. Weston and Bernheim hired Wilder and Izzy Diamond to prepare an Americanised rewrite for Lemmon and Matthau.

Wilder expressed the hope that *Buddy, Buddy* would be, 'a bit like *Some Like It Hot*, and hopefully it'll be fast and funny. But unlike *Kiss Me Stupid* this is a commercial movie – nothing arty in it, nothing very serious, somewhere between *Stir Crazy* and George Bernard

Shaw.' Lemmon even went on record in the *Hollywood Reporter* saying, 'It's the funniest script I've read since *Some Like It Hot.'*

Principal photography began on 4 February at MGM Studios in Culver City with location filming to come in Santa Monica, the County Courthouse in Riverside and Hawaii. By all accounts the atmosphere on set was like a carnival as an easy, working shorthand had developed between the trio of workers and friends. Jay Weston marvelled, 'Wilder only has to give an indication of what he wants and they know.' Izzy Diamond observed that Wilder's directorial style now allowed a 'little flexibility' to Matthau. Everyone joked and toiled their way through what seemed a sure-fire hit.

It was during the making of *The Fortune Cookie* that Matthau had suffered his heart attack. He had escaped any harm on *The Front Page* but wasn't so lucky on *Buddy, Buddy*. One scene called for Lemmon and Matthau to hurl themselves feet first down a laundry chute. When Matthau came down he bounced off the mattress that was supposed to soften his fall and cracked the back of his head on a cement floor. Wilder later recalled, 'I must be an ogre or a tyrant or something with all these terrible things that happen to him on my films. He could have had a stuntman but he was just fooling around when he fell. I thought he was dead. We were all stunned and nobody moved except Jack who rushed over and held him. Walter looked up and said, "Jack, it's curtains for me." It was like a line from a B-picture, Edward G. Robinson or something. I couldn't help but laugh.' Matthau spent only a few days in hospital before the production moved on to Hawaii and completed filming.

Wilder was typically enthusiastic about his stars: 'Redford, Beatty, Reynolds; they're all talented and popular but they're interchangeable, anonymous actors.

Matthau is a unique star. When you write a script for him – or for Lemmon – there is no possible alternative to him. He's very uniquely distinctive – he has a walk all his own and a face all his own. Matthau is a palette with every colour you want. He has enough talent to make four big stars. He's as deft at comedy as he is at drama.

'He is a good actor, very economical. He knows how to get the maximum out of close-ups. For all the trouble and aggravation he puts me through, I wish I could have him for my next fifty pictures.'

Unfortunately, the enthusiasm which the stars and director felt for the film was not shared by critics or the public. Hardly anyone at all came to see *Buddy, Buddy,* released in America for the Christmas season in 1981. In the film Matthau is Trabucco, a hit-man hired to dispose of three witnesses scheduled to testify in a land fraud case. His 'pest control' runs smoothly until he crosses the path of one Victor Clooney (Lemmon), a neurotic television censor intent on regaining the hand of his estranged wife Cecilia (Paula Prentiss) who has virtually defected to a sex clinic run by Dr Zuckerbrot (Klaus Kinski). Trabucco and Clooney find themselves in adjoining hotel rooms and that's when the trouble begins. Clooney finally realises that Cecilia has no interest in returning to him and tries to commit suicide. His various botched attempts distract, disturb and enrage Trabucco who is lining up his rifle sights to eliminate his final victim.

Eventually, through a tangle of complications, Trabucco attempts to reunite Victor and Cecilia (to no avail) whilst Victor pulls the trigger that completes the task in hand for his best buddy. Going their separate ways Trabucco heads for a remote, idyllic island paradise away from all worries and bothersome strangers. However, one day a small boat crashes onto the reef surrounding the island. There is one lone figure in the boat – Victor.

Buddy, Buddy presents Lemmon and Matthau in their familiar Wilder guises; Lemmon as the down-trodden shmuck, unlucky in love and desperate for affection, with the personality of a lovable pup that will soil the carpet to gain attention. Matthau is morose and petty with Machiavellian schemes in mind and scant regard for his fellow human beings. The actors are comfortable and accomplished within their roles but the film just doesn't work. It lacks the necessary pace for a freewheeling farce, the characters seem thinly sketched and cardboard-like compared to the richness of *The Fortune Cookie*, the victims chosen for the Wilder-Diamond jokes (hippies and sex clinics) are old-fashioned and the film has a lazy sixties feel to it.

The prospect of Lemmon and Matthau reading the telephone book is an attractive one and a film with their particular chemistry couldn't lack at least incidental pleasures – even *Buddy, Buddy* had its share of those. Matthau's blackhearted, business-bent, cigar-chomping hit-man has a penchant for disguise and thus the actor is a postman, milkman and Irish priest within the space of an hour and a half. One scene calls for him to deliver the last rites to a dying man and the dialogue is a mixture of all the Latin phrases he can remember: *'Tempus fugit e habeas corpus cave canem e flagrante delicto.'* Matthau's expressive rubber features are put to good effect and milk the most from some situations, never more so than when faced with the increasingly blood-boiling nuisance of Lemmon's Clooney to whom he must remain courteous to keep up an appearance of normalcy when the bellboy is around. He pleads that Clooney is entitled to, 'a little human warmth' while the murderous gleam in his eyes suggests the exact opposite.

Despite some good moments, *Buddy, Buddy* was savaged by the press and failed to recover its production costs on its American release. The fun of the filming and alleged quality of the script had somehow failed to translate onto the screen. Lemmon tactfully believed that the finished article was 'not everything we hoped for midway through production'.

Matthau was now at the stage in his career where the dilemma was, what to do next. He wasn't enthusiastic about doing just another comedy, it had to be something special. *Buddy, Buddy* had appeared to fit that criteria but the results can only have disappointed. 'Deciding what to do next becomes more and more difficult as I get older,' he said in a 1981 newspaper interview. 'These days there have to be very compelling reasons for me to do a film. Years ago it used to be a lark, acting. Not any more. Now it's just hard work.'

Early in 1982 the nominations for the Golden Globe awards were announced in Hollywood. Matthau had been nominated for Best Actor in a Comedy for his work in *The First Monday in October* with Jill Clayburgh nominated as Best Actress. Film executives were soon floating the idea of a sequel that would reteam the stars. Matthau displayed a similar speed in quashing the idea: 'That's not for me. I abhor the idea of doing sequels. Do that and you might as well be in a television series.' When the Golden Globes were awarded several weeks later Dudley Moore was voted the Best Actor in a Comedy for *Arthur* in which he played a booze-befuddled millionaire.

Matthau chose to stay on familiar ground with his next project – Neil Simon's *I Ought to Be in Pictures* directed by Herbert Ross. Matthau plays Herb Tucker, a Hollywood screenwriter who is one day visited by his nineteen-year-old daughter Libby (Dinah Manoff) whom he has not seen since he abandoned her and the rest of the family sixteen years previously. Libby wants to make a career as an actress but Herb isn't quite the success that everyone thought him to be. But he does have a warm, loving relationship with Steffie (Ann-Margret), a hairdresser at one of the major studios. The estranged father and daughter fight, argue and generally dislike each other until a mutual understanding develops and a common bond is uncovered.

I Ought to Be in Pictures went the same way as *Buddy, Buddy* and received a resounding thumbs down from both the public and the critics. The Neil Simon laughter machine found itself stuck in a groove of contrived predictability. The play (which originally had Tony Curtis in the lead) had been a Broadway success with Dinah Manoff winning a Tony award. The film was a flop, earning a measly four million dollars in domestic rentals and an unexpectedly bad status as one of the year's top box-office losers. Writing in the *New York Times*, Vincent Canby didn't spare the punches: '. . . I found it unbearable. Being so mechanical, so slick and so sentimental, it is, at heart, heartless, and though it has the hyped-up pacing one associates with Broadway, it seems longer than Nicholas Nickelby. *I Ought to Be in Pictures* ought not to be.' To date the film has not been seen in Britain.

Two expensive flops in a row gave Matthau pause for reflection. He took a break from work, followed other interests and socialised. He was a popular presenter at the 1982 Oscar ceremony, being on hand with Jack Lemmon to deliver a perfectly timed and witty treatise on directors before placing the Best Director's Award in the hands of Warren Beatty. He was back the following year as one of the four masters of ceremonies. That year Jack Lemmon was in the audience, nominated in the

Best Actor category for his performance in *Missing* as an American father in search of his missing son in Latin America. Matthau's friend Billy Wilder presented the Best Director Award to Richard Attenborough. Matthau himself was seen at the opening of the fifty-fifth annual ceremony singing (rather uncomfortably) the un-memorable ditty 'The Moment of Truth is Here' alongside his fellow hosts for the evening, Liza Minnelli, Dudley Moore and Richard Pryor. Matthau joked with Sylvester Stallone and introduced Carol Burnett but Minnelli admitted that the four hosts had more fun together backstage than before the cameras.

In the self-imposed lull in his schedule he toured the Middle East with Carol and Jack and Felicia Lemmon. However, by 1983 his interest was awakened by a comedy script that he really wanted to do – *The Survivors*. A satire with something to say about contemporary America, *The Survivors* was directed by Michael Ritchie and released for the summer of 1983 from a screenplay by Michael Leeson, a veteran of the *Taxi* television series.

The film's producer William Sackheim was responsible for the original idea which stemmed from his interest in survivorship. 'These people flee to the hills, and once they get up there, they don't trust anybody – including each other. There's a kind of madness about it. Somehow it struck me as a very funny idea for a comedy.' Matthau's co-star Robin Williams stated, 'I wanted to do a far-out comedy. I like the basic premise – if we stick together it will all work out. It's sort of like Yin, Yang and Yong. You've got me, who, I guess, specialises in frenetic and bizarre energy. You've got Walter Matthau, who's very grounded and subtle. And then you've got Jerry Reed, whose character is like a cross between Mister Rogers and Jack Nicholson. He's a lovable villain.'

The Survivors are attempting to cope with the bleak economy and the blight of unemployment. Matthau is Sonny Paluso, a gas station owner whose establishment goes up in flames when a cigarette butt is thrown in the wrong direction. Williams is Donald Quinelle, a sales executive who not only faces the ignominy of being sacked but receives the news from the boss's pet parrot. Reed is hired-gun Jack Locke who discovers that even the mob isn't immune to the cutbacks of hard times. Attempting to drown his sorrows with a simple cup of coffee at the luncheonette where he meets Sonny, Donald is held up by masked gunman Locke but foils the robbery and becomes a TV hero. Locke is now forced to consider eliminating Donald and Sonny as witnesses to his crime. Donald however has become carried away with his role as a solid, upstanding citizen and becomes a recruit in a private army. He is all set for a showdown with Locke but can't go through with it; he has the wrong bullets for his armoury. Sonny remains level-headed and sane about the whole business – he thinks Jack has gone off his rocker. Eventually a union of Sonny, Donald and Jack materialises to defeat the right-wing military unit with which Donald has become entangled.

The Survivors received some excellent reviews and must have reaffirmed Matthau's faith that there was an audience for the 'candy' pictures. It wasn't just a hilarious comedy but a film with a point of view on the morality of Reaganite America that can't have failed to appeal to Matthau's liberal sentiments. *Time* magazine assessed the film as a success: '*The Survivors* is the summer's only true satire, a mostly-successful attempt to puncture a ballooning national lunacy with pinpricks of beleagured rationalism . . . . Matthau, stooped and shuffling under the burden of his sanity (has) his richest part in years.' The latter words can only have been music to the ears of a man beset by self-doubt and while the film was not a smash hit the domestic rentals amassed were in excess of twenty million dollars.

Chapter Twelve

What kind of person is Walter Matthau? On screen his 'star' persona has become that of the lovable grouch; gruff and cynical but more often than not with a heart of gold. That has become the Walter Matthau 'type' with which audiences identify. Off-screen he appears to adopt the same character with a wisecrack for every occasion and the desire not to take anything too seriously, particularly himself. Yet this character is something of a smoke-screen, a convenience used to disguise the worries, anguish and sensitivity of a shy, shrewd and intelligent man.

'There are two misconceptions about me: one that I'm an extrovert, and two that horse racing is my real passion in life,' he has said. 'Sure I gamble – but not to the exclusion of all else. People also think I own race horses. False again.

'There's something about people who own horses that doesn't appeal to me. They tend to treat human beings as though they own them as well, and that's a very unpleasant characteristic. This reputation I have of being a massive punter is getting out of hand. I go to the opera much more often than I go to the races. Just because I spent a large part of my early movie career playing inarticulate heavies, it doesn't mean to say I'm uncultured. I went to a performance of *The Tales of*

Hoffman and an actress I know came up to me and said, "Why Walter, what are you doing here?" I said, "I'm waiting for the next bus to take me to the race-track." She was a bit put out I guess. But then so was I.'

He has expressed the view that, 'There must be an enormous tragic button in the head of an actor for him to be able to do comedy.' Perhaps gambling has been his own button; certainly over the years it is an addiction which has cost him a fortune. 'I am no longer a compulsive gambler,' he was able to say in the seventies. 'I now gamble willingly and place lower wagers. I will bet a hundred dollars a game with Billy (Wilder). The Los Angeles Dodgers don't mean a damn thing to me, or the Rams, unless I have money on them.' This didn't mean that there wasn't the odd occasion on which he went over the top. 'I was at the race track last Sunday,' he said in 1976, 'sitting next to Cary Grant in the directors' room where they give you, free, eighteen different kinds of chicken, steak and veal. I was betting twenty dollars a race till I saw something I liked in the seventh. I put $1000 on it. It was nipped at the wire. I bet $2000 on the last and it was caught by an absent-minded seven-to-one shot. Cary never bet more than two dollars.'

He is certainly firm in his stance about not extending his interest to horse-owning. 'They offered me a horse to buy but I said no. You want to know what the name of that horse is? Telly's Pop – it belongs to Telly Savalas and Howard Koch and it has won every race you can think of. Telly and Howard paid six thousand dollars for the nag after I turned down the offer. The horse made $300,000 so far. That goes to show you what kind of gambler I am. If I had bought him, the poor thing would have lost every race.'

When his reputation as a reckless, indiscriminate gambler was becoming too much to bear he pointed out,

'This reputation I have for betting on anything, that is absolutely fallacious. Like which of the two flies will climb a wall faster. I don't make fly-on-the-wall bets. I don't make will-it-rain-tomorrow bets. I bet on baseball, football, basketball and horses. I like to win. It is not true that the real gambler wants to lose – but losing, it hurts more than winning, and a pain is a more dramatic emotion than a pleasure. For losing to give you this drama, it has to be unbearable, and you have to make sure you lose enough to hurt.'

Attempts to divine the cause of his gambling fever usually flounder on a re-adoption by Matthau of his comic mask. The extreme poverty of his childhood or his personal insecurities must have at least led him on to the gambling path. He does admit to seeking the counsel of a psychiatrist, and joked in a 1976 interview, 'Saw two. One was a compulsive eater, weighed 400lbs and smoked six different pipes during the fifty-minute session.

'The other, I had to hammer on his door for ten minutes. Finally, he unbolted it and said, "Come in, come in, my friend, my door is always open".' He was still skirting the issue with a protective layer of humour in a further interview four years later, by which time he had refined the psychiatrist story thus, 'On the one occasion in my life that I went to see a psychiatrist, fifteen minutes after meeting the guy he suggested we become partners in a bookmaking concern!

'I'd gone to him with some personal problems that had absolutely nothing to do with horses – but there was no way he was going to take me seriously. Actually, I can't really blame him. When I phoned to make the appointment, I told his secretary I was Jean Valjean from *Les Miserables* and that I was coming round to return the candlesticks.'

For Matthau, it seems, humour can always hide the hurt.

His gambling never seems to have been a cause for dissent in his enduring marriage to Carol, one-time débutante and now a retired actress; a writer, formidable socialiser and a strong personality who will have been Mrs Matthau for twenty-five years in 1984. In a published extract from Truman Capote's novel *Answered Prayers*, Carol and her friend Gloria Vanderbilt Cooper are described as, 'two charmingly incompetent adventuresses'. Capote quotes a lunchtime conversation between the two:

Mrs Matthau: 'I never imagined I'd marry an actor. Well, marry perhaps. But not for love. Yet here I've been stuck with Walter all these years and it still makes me curdle if I see his eye stray a fraction. Have you seen this new Swedish girl called Karen something?'

Mrs Cooper: 'Wasn't she in some spy picture?'

Mrs Matthau: 'Exactly. Lovely face. Divine photographed from the bazooms up. But the legs are strictly redwood forest. Anyway we met her at the Widmarks and she was moving her eyes around and making all these little noises for Walter's benefit. I stood it as long as I could, but when I heard Walter say, "How old are you, Karen?" I said, "For God's sake, Walter, why don't you chop off her legs and read the rings?"'

Billy Wilder has commented that he can turn up for dinner and find that Carol has just finished lunch with Felicia Lemmon, such is her prodigious ability to enjoy social events.

Carol has also voiced her opinions on her husband's career with both success and failure but usually to some effect. She thought that *The Odd Couple* was less than wonderful and, when proved spectacularly wrong, promised herself never to voice an opinion again. She broke that promise when she read the script for *Kotch* and was so convinced of its worth that she persuaded Matthau to read it and he went on to receive an Oscar nomination for the part. After *The Odd Couple* Carol insisted that Matthau quadruple his asking price. 'Me? I'd have been happy just to double it,' says Matthau.

Asked in a 1979 interview about his wife Matthau replied, 'I don't think I give her enough security. I think there's a lot of bastard in me. I'll hold a grudge too long. Carol asked me where I was last night and I said, "At the game". She said, "Ray Stark called for you and he said there was no game". I said, "For chrissake Carol, that's Ray Stark's idea of a joke". I was being questioned. Me! The last faithful husband on the face of the planet!'

Carol has also been responsible for involving Matthau in the Hollywood social scene, sometimes forcing him to parties against his introvert nature. He can usually predict the results. 'When I take Carol to parties everyone says: "You look marvellous, Carol" and "How do you do it Carol?" Nobody says a word to me. They just look at me and I know what they're thinking. "God – he looks awful. Another six months at most."'

Carol has been with him through the lean years and the successful ones, supportive and individualistic. Not too many Hollywood couples reach their silver-wedding anniversary, as Carol and Walter will in 1984.

Matthau's story is virtually the classic tale of rags (and gags) to riches. The scenario of a poor kid from a tough New York neighbourhood rising to be a highly-paid, world-renowned movie star is the American Dream writ large. (His brother, Henry, was a success at a more modest level in the Army-Navy surplus business in New York.) However, nothing is ever as simple as that. Stardom was a long time arriving and there were years of struggle, anonymity and uncertainty before he was established. Stardom too has brought its drawbacks and Matthau has seldom been reluctant to bite the hand that feeds, carping at the restrictions placed on the working perimeters of a movie star. A tiny part of him yearns for the 'living on the brink' days of the fifties with masses of various characters to illuminate on stage, in television and on film. Mostly, he realises that those days are gone, that he plays comedy superbly and that, if he is rarely allowed to stray from this territory, then it is the price he has to pay. It doesn't stop him from striking out occasionally and agents have proved a perennial target; on *The Sunshine Boys* he claims that he was advised that once he played an old Jew the public wouldn't want to see him as anything else. 'I have an agent who is expert in knowing what's rotten. Sometimes, of course, we disagree. In fact I've made a point of saving all the letters where he has said something's no good and the film has gone on to make thirty million dollars. One day I'll throw that at him.' When one Hollywood producer criticised one of his performances Matthau told him, 'Well, it was a crappy part in a crappy movie for a crappy studio with a crappy executive. Thank you and goodnight.'

Despite the jokey exterior and the cracks about 'retirement acting' he cares deeply about his craft and the tradition of screen comedy and is one of its best contemporary exponents. He has taken part in the celebration film tributes to Chaplin in *The Gentleman Tramp* (1975) and other laughter-makers like W.C. Fields, the Marx Brothers and Laurel and Hardy in the television compilations *Funny Business* (1978) and *Hollywood: The Gift of Laughter* (1982). His dedication is revealed in the following quote: 'When producers say, I want a Walter Matthau role of a Matthau project, they're limiting me, and it's curtains for me as an artist. And when they say they see me as a comedian, only a comedian, they don't know what they're talking about, because the one thing I'm most serious about is my comedy. Comedy is tougher than tragedy. Comedy is not the opposite of drama. Comedy is a sub-heading of drama, and tragedy is the other main sub-heading. At the end of a day shooting a comedy film, I'm drained.'

The move from New York to Los Angeles, and the career shift from stage to film was not embarked upon lightly but Matthau has mellowed in his attitudes. In the seventies he revealed, 'I succumbed to the movies in 1955 because I needed the money. I was always happiest working on the stage. But now plays are a sort of outmoded thing. You can say all the dirty words in films. There aren't that many good plays around, and I can't stand mediocrity. Besides, the big money is in Hollywood.' More recently still he said, 'I had a heart attack at a very early age so I decided to take it easy and stay out in California. I put on my shorts this morning and went into the ocean. I took a five-mile walk, which I do three or four times a week. You just can't do that in New York.'

He has also been exceptionally encouraging to the children that are following in his footsteps, employing David, Charlie and Carol's daughter Lucy in many of his films. 'I'm a nepot,' he cheerfully admits. The man cares deeply, despite anything he may say to the contrary. Neil Simon has called him one of the top two or three actors in America – 'he can make you cry with one tenth of his talent', while Jack Lemmon believes: 'He has talent that still hasn't been tapped. Films haven't yet touched on his depths.' Matthau himself can be more circumspect about his career: 'I know they say Matthau looks better than his material. I've done fifty-odd pictures and forty-five have made money. But I've been semi-satisfied with maybe a half-dozen.'

Now in his sixties Matthau's strong liberalism can only be disheartened at the static nature of events in his own country where some still experience the poverty he endured as a child. There's more than a touch of sadness in the following comments: 'When I look in the mirror I think: that man is an old man. His hair is still dark but he is old. Well, I can live with that. What's difficult to live with is my disappointment in the slow progress of people in realising that the only worthwhile thing on this planet is the arts. Books, music, films, theatre – they are what's important, not whether some guy makes fifty million dollars.

'That's not what the planet is all about: that's not what we crawled out of the primeval sludge to celebrate. But money is all some people seem to talk about these days. Soon it will be: "How do you do? How much money do you make?"

'Then there's sex. That's got to the point where some men now say to girls: "How old are you? Do you want to make love?"

'I did this once, as a joke, to see if it would work. And it did. It terrified me. The girl grabbed me. "No, No," I said. "I was just showing off my new freedom, my liberation from the shackles of ignorance, despair and darkness." "Oh," she said, disappointed. "I thought you were serious."'

Matthau is even uncomfortable with some of the elements in his own complex make-up. His Jewish background left him with a permanent raw nerve regarding all thing German. Yet he has been seen driving a large scarlet Mercedes with the number plate WALTZ. He explained: 'The studio gave it to me and when I refused it, they said I was prejudiced against it because it was German. As I hate Germany because of its prejudice, I realised they were right so I took it.'

Comic, convoluted, intelligent and perceptive, Walter Matthau treats life as a cabaret and he has more than earned the right to do so. Facing the adversities as well as the triumphs of life with a laugh is one of the best self-defence strategies in the world. The contradictions of his character, of a shy introvert, a self-critical success and a genuinely caring, shop-soiled cynic are best summed up in his own phrase, 'I'm insecure and I thrive on it.'

As to the future, he would probably still like to win the Best Actor Oscar; it would be physical proof of what his colleagues believe: that he is one of the best in the business. He has declared his intent, with Carol, to 'stay alive and beat the system so I can keep some of the money I've earned'.

To end on an entirely appropriate note, he has voiced one further ambition: 'I want to do Macbeth – naked.'

The Films of
Walter Matthau

THE KENTUCKIAN (1955)
A Hecht-Lancaster Production. Director: Burt Lancaster.
Producer: Harold Hecht. Screenplay: A. B. Guthrie Jnr
from the novel *The Gabriel Horn* by Felix Holt.
Photography: Ernest Laszlo. 104 minutes.
Cast: Burt Lancaster, Dianne Foster, Diana Lynn, John
McIntire, Una Merkel, Walter Matthau, John Carradine,
Donald MacDonald, John Litel, Rhys Williams.

Matthau as whip-brandishing tavern-owner Sam
Bodine.

THE INDIAN FIGHTER (1955)
A Bryna Production. Director: Andre de Toth. Producer:
William Schorr. Screenplay: Frank Davis and Ben Hecht
from a story by Ben Kadish. Photography: Wilfrid M.
Cline. 88 minutes.
Cast: Kirk Douglas, Elsa Martinelli, Walter Abel, Walter
Matthau, Diana Douglas, Eduard Franz, Lon Chaney
Jnr, Alan Hale Jnr, Elisha Cook Jnr, Michael Winkelman,
Harry Landers.

Matthau as chief villain Wes Todd.

BIGGER THAN LIFE (1956)
A Twentieth Century-Fox Production. Director:
Nicholas Ray. Producer: James Mason. Screenplay:

Clifford Odets and Nicholas Ray from an original story by Cyril Hume and Richard Maibaum. Photography: Joe MacDonald. 95 minutes.

Cast: James Mason, Barbara Rush, Walter Matthau, Robert Simon, Christopher Olsen, Roland Winters, Rusty Lane, Rachel Stephens, Kipp Hamilton, Betty Caulfield.

Matthau as family friend, gym teacher Wally Gibbs.

A FACE IN THE CROWD (1957)

A Newton Production. Director/Producer: Elia Kazan. Screenplay: Budd Schulberg from his story *Our Arkansas Traveller*. Photography: Harry Stradling and Gayne Rescher. 126 minutes.

Cast: Andy Griffith, Patricia Neal, Anthony Franciosa, Walter Matthau, Lee Remick, Percy Waram, Marshall Neilan, Kay Medford.

Matthau as cynical writer Mel Miller, the 'other' man.

SLAUGHTER ON TENTH AVENUE (1957)

A Universal-International Production. Director: Arnold Laven. Producer: Albert Zugsmith. Screenplay: Lawrence Roman from the novel *The Man Who Rocked the Boat* by William J. Keating and Richard Carter. Photography: Fred Jackman. 103 minutes.

Cast: Richard Egan, Jan Sterling, Dan Duryea, Julie Adams, Walter Matthau, Charles McGraw, Sam Levene, Mickey Shaughnessy, Harry Bellaver, Nick Dennis, Ned Weaver.

Matthau as Al Dahlke waterfront king-pin.

KING CREOLE (1958)

A Paramount Production. Director: Michael Curtiz. Producer: Hal B. Wallis. Screenplay: Herbert Baker and Michael V. Gazzo from the novel *A Stone for Danny Fisher*

by Harold Robbins. Photography: Russell Harlan. 116 minutes.
Cast: Elvis Presley, Carolyn Jones, Dolores Hart, Dean Jagger, Walter Matthau, Lillian Montevicchi, Vic Morrow, Jan Shepherd, Paul Stewart, Brian Hutton, Jack Grinnage.

Matthau as nightclub-owner Maxie Fields.

VOICE IN THE MIRROR (1958)

A Universal-International Production. Director: Harry Keller. Producer: Gordon Kay. Screenplay: Larry Marcus. Photography: William Daniels. 102 minutes.
Cast: Richard Egan, Julie London, Arthur O'Connell, Walter Matthau, Troy Donahue, Harry Bartell, Peggy Converse, Ann Doran, Mae Clarke, Casey Adams*, Hugh Sanders.

Matthau as orthodox medical practitioner Dr Leon Karnes.

RIDE A CROOKED TRAIL (1958)

A Universal-International Production. Director: Jesse Hibbs, Producer: Howard Pine. Screenplay: Borden Chase from a story by George Bruce. 87 minutes.
Cast: Audie Murphy, Gia Scala, Walter Matthau, Henry Silva, Joanna Moore, Eddie Little, Mary Field, Leo Gordon, Mort Mills, Frank Chase, Bill Walker, Ned Weaver.

Matthau as Judge Kyle, law officer in Little Rock.

ONIONHEAD (1958)

A Warner Brothers Production. Director: Norman Taurog. Producer: Jules Schermer. Screenplay: Nelson Gidding from the novel by Weldon Hill. Photography: Harold Rosson. 110 minutes.

*later known as Max Showalter

Cast: Andy Griffith, Felicia Farr, Walter Matthau, Erin O'Brien, Joe Mantell, Ray Danton, Roscoe Karns, James Gregory, Tige Andrews, Joey Bishop, Claude Akins, Ainslie Pryor.

Matthau as overbearing ship's cook Red Wildoe.

Gangster Story (1959)

An Independent Producers Production. Director: Walter Matthau. Producer: Jonathan Daniels. Screenplay: Paul Purcell from an original story by Richard Grey and V.J. Rhems. 70 minutes.

Cast: Walter Mathau, Carol Grace, Bruce McFarlan, Garrett Wallberg, Raiken Ben Ari.

Matthau as doomed criminal genius Jack Martin.

Strangers When We Meet (1960)

A Bryna-Quine Production. Director/Producer: Richard Quine. Screenplay: Evan Hunter from his own novel. Photography: Charles Lang Jnr. 117 minutes.

Cast: Kirk Douglas, Kim Novak, Ernie Kovacs, Barbara Rush, Walter Matthau, Virginia Bruce, Kent Smith, Helen Gallagher, John Bryant, Roberta Shore, Nancy Kovak, Carol Douglas.

Matthau as lecherous neighbourhood wolf Felix Anders.

Lonely Are the Brave (1962)

A Joel (Kirk Douglas) Production. Director: David Miller. Producer: Edward Lewis. Screenplay: Dalton Trumbo from the novel *Brave Cowboy* by Edward Abbey. Photography: Philip Lathrop. 107 minutes.

Cast: Kirk Douglas, Gena Rowlands, Walter Matthau, Michael Kane, Carroll O'Connor, William Schallert, Karl Swenson, George Kennedy, Dan Sheridan, Bill Raisch.

Matthau as the laconic Sheriff Johnson.

WHO'S GOT THE ACTION? (1962)
A Paramount-Amro Production. Director: Daniel Mann.
Producer: Jack Rose. Screenplay: Jack Rose from the
novel *Four Horse Players Are Missing* by Alexander Rose.
Photography: Joseph Ruttenberg. 93 minutes.
Cast: Dean Martin, Lana Turner, Eddie Albert, Walter
Matthau, Nita Talbot, Margo, Paul Ford, John McGiver,
Jack Albertson.

Matthau as racketeer Tony Gagoots.

ISLAND OF LOVE (1963)
A Belgrave Enterprises Production. Director/Producer:
Morton da Costa. Screenplay: David R. Shwarz from a
story by Leo Katcher. Photography: Harry Stradling. 101
minutes.
Cast: Robert Preston, Tony Randall, Walter Matthau,
Georgia Moll, Betty Bruce.

Matthau as Brooklyn gangster Tony Dallas.

CHARADE (1963)
A Universal-International Production. Director/Pro-
ducer: Stanley Donen. Screenplay: Peter Stone from
a story by Peter Stone and Marc Behm. Photography:
Charles Lang Jnr. 113 minutes.
Cast: Cary Grant, Audrey Hepburn, Walter Matthau,
James Coburn, George Kennedy, Ned Glass, Jacques
Marin, Paul Bonifas, Dominique Minot, Thomas
Chelimsky.

Matthau as Hamilton Bartholomew treacherous 'CIA
chief'.

ENSIGN PULVER (1964)
A Warner Brothers Production. Director/Producer:
Joshua Logan. Screenplay: Joshua Logan and Peter S.
Feibleman from the original play by Joshua Logan and

Thomas Heggen. Photography: Charles Lawton. 104 minutes.
Cast: Robert Walker Jnr, Burl Ives, Walter Matthau, Tommy Sands, Millie Perkins, Kay Medford, Larry Hagman, Gerald O'Laughlin, Al Freeman Jnr, James Ferentino, Jack Nicholson, Diana Sands, Sal Papa, James Coco.

Matthau as the ship's worldy-wise Doc.

GOODBYE CHARLIE (1964)
A Twentieth Century-Fox/Venice Production. Director: Vincente Minnelli. Producer: David Weisbart. Screenplay: Harry Kurnitz from the play by George Axelrod. Photography: Milton Krasner. 116 minutes.
Cast: Tony Curtis, Debbie Reynolds, Pat Boone, Walter Matthau, Ellen MacRae*, Joanna Barnes, Laura Devon.

Matthau as Hungarian film producer Sir Leopold Sartori.

FAIL SAFE (1964)
A Columbia Production. Director: Sidney Lumet. Producer: Max E. Youngstein. Screenplay: Walter Bernstein from the novel by Eugene Burdick and Harvey Wheeler. Photography: Gerald Hirschfeld. 111 minutes.
Cast: Henry Fonda, Walter Matthau, Dan O'Herlihy, Frank Overton, Fritz Weaver, Edward Binns, Larry Hagman, Russell Collins, Dom de Luise.

Matthau as Groeteschele, hawkish civilian adviser to the government.

MIRAGE (1965)
A Universal-International Production. Director: Edward Dmytryk. Producer: Harry Keller. Screenplay: Peter Stone from the novel by Howard Fast. Photography: Joe MacDonald. 109 minutes.

* later known as Ellen Burstyn.

Cast: Gregory Peck, Diane Baker, Walter Matthau, Walter Abel, Leif Erickson, Kevin McCarthy, Anne Seymour, Jack Weston, George Kennedy.

Matthau as easy-going private detective Ted Caselle.

THE FORTUNE COOKIE (1966) (UK:Meet Whiplash Willie)
A Phalanx-Jalem Production. Director/Producer: Billy Wilder. Screenplay: Billy Wilder and I.A.L. Diamond. Photography: Joseph La Shelle. 125 minutes.
Cast: Jack Lemmon, Walter Matthau, Judi West, Ron Rich, Marge Redmond, Lurene Tuttle, Cliff Osmond, Noam Pitlik, Harry Holcombe, Les Tremayne, Sig Ruman.

Matthau as unscrupulous lawyer Willie Gingrich.

A GUIDE FOR THE MARRIED MAN (1967)
A Twentieth Century-Fox Production. Director: Gene Kelly. Producer: Frank McCarthy. Screenplay: Frank Tarloff from his book. Photography: Joe MacDonald. 89 minutes.
Cast: Walter Matthau, Robert Morse, Inger Stevens, Sue Ann Langdon, Clair Kelly, Lind Harrison, Elaine Devry.
Guests: Lucille Ball, Jack Benny, Polly Bergen, Joey Biship, Sid Caesar, Art Carney, Jeffrey Hunter, Sam Jaffe, Jayne Mansfield, Carl Reiner, Phil Silvers, Terry-Thomas.

Matthau as Paul Manning, the 'married man'.

THE ODD COUPLE (1968)
A Howard W. Koch Production. Director: Gene Saks. Producer: Howard W. Koch. Screenplay: Neil Simon from his own play. Photography: Robert B. Hauser. 105 minutes.
Cast: Jack Lemmon, Walter Matthau, Monica Evans, Carole Shelley, David Sheiner, A. Larry Haines, John Fielder, Herbert Edelman.

Matthau as the supremely slovenly sports commentator, Oscar Madison.

THE SECRET LIFE OF AN AMERICAN WIFE (1968)
A Charlton Production. Director/Producer/Screenplay: George Axelrod. Photography: Leon Shamroy. 92 minutes.
Cast: Walter Matthau, Anne Jackson, Patrick O'Neal, Edy Williams, Richard Bull, Paul Napier.
Matthau as the world famous 'movie star'.

CANDY (1968)
A Selmur/Dear/Corona Production. Director: Christian Marquand. Producer: Robert Haggiag. Screenplay: Buck Henry from the novel by Terry Southern and Mason Hoffenburg. Photography: Giuseppe Rotunno. 124 minutes.
Cast: Ewa Aulin, Charles Aznavour, Marlon Brando, Richard Burton, James Coburn, John Huston, Walter Matthau, Ringo Starr, John Astin, Elsa Martinelli, Sugar Ray Robinson.
Matthau as the bomb-happy General Smight.

HELLO DOLLY (1969)
A Chenault Production. Director: Gene Kelly. Producer/Screenplay: Ernest Lehman. Photography: Harry Stradling. 129 minutes.
Cast: Barbra Streisand, Walter Matthau, Michael Crawford, Louis Armstrong, Marianne McAndrew, E.J. Peaker, Danny Lockin, Joyce Ames, Tommy Tune, Judy Knaiz, David Hurst.
Matthau as wealthy merchant Horace Vandergelder.

CACTUS FLOWER (1969)
A Columbia Production. Director: Gene Saks. Producer:

Mike J. Frankovich. Screenplay: I.A.L. Diamond from the play by Abe Burrows. Photography: Charles E. Lang. 103 minutes.
Cast: Ingrid Bergman, Walter Matthau, Goldie Hawn, Jack Weston, Rick Lenz, Vito Scotti, Irne Hervey, Eve Bruce, Irwin Charone, Matthew Saks.

Matthau as marriage-shy dentist Julian Winston.

New Leaf (1970)
An Aries-Elkin Production. Director/Screenplay: Elaine May from the short story *The Green Heart* by Jack Ritchie. Producer: Joe Manduke. Photography: Gayne Rescher. 102 minutes.
Cast: Walter Matthau, Elaine May, Jack Weston, George Rose, William Redfield, James Coco, Graham Jarvis, Doris Roberts, Rose Arrick, Renee Taylor, Mark Gordon, Jess Osuna.

Matthau as Henry Graham, impoverished member of the idle rich.

Plaza Suite (1971)
A Paramount Production. Director: Arthur Hiller. Producer: Howard W. Koch. Screenplay: Neil Simon from his play. Photography: Jack Marta. 114 minutes.
Cast: Walter Matthau, Maureen Stapleton, Barbara Harris, Lee Grant, Louise Sorel, Jennie Sullivan, Tom Carey, Jose Ocasio, Dan Ferrone.

Matthau as businessman Sam Noah, movie producer Jesse Kiplinger and irate, father-of-the bride Roy Hubley.

Kotch (1971)
A Kotch Company Production. Director: Jack Lemmon. Producer: Richard Carter. Screenplay: John Paxton from the novel by Katherine Tompkins. Photography: Richard H. Kline. 114 minutes.

Cast: Walter Matthau, Deborah Winters, Felicia Farr, Charles Aidman, Ellen Geer, James Brohead, Jane Connell, Jessica Rains, Paul Picerni, Darrel Larson, Larry Linville, Arlen Stuart.
Matthau as septuagenarian Joseph P. Kotcher.

PETE'N'TILLIE (1972)

A Universal Production. Director: Martin Ritt. Producer/Screenplay: Julius J. Epstein from the novella *Witch's Milk* by Peter de Vries. Photography: John Alonzo. 100 minutes.
Cast: Walter Matthau, Carol Burnett, Geraldine Page, Barry Nelson, Rene Auberjonois, Lee Montgomery, Henry Jones, Kent Smith, Philip Bourneauf, Whit Bissell, Timothy Blake.
Matthau as gregarious bachelor Pete.

CHARLEY VARRICK (1973)

A Universal Production. Director/Producer: Don Siegel. Screenplay: Howard Rodman and Dean Reisner from the novel *The Looters* by John Reese. Photography: Michael Butler. 111 minutes.
Cast: Walter Matthau, Joe Don Baker, Felicia Farr, Andy Robinson, John Vernon, Sheree North, Norman Fell, Benson Fong, Woodrow Parfrey, William Schallert, Jacqueline Scott, Charlie Matthau.
Matthau as small-time robber Charley Varrick.

THE LAUGHING POLICEMAN (1973) (UK: An Investigation of Murder)

A Twentieth Century-Fox Production. Director/Producer: Stuart Rosenberg. Screenplay: Thomas Rickman from the novel by Per Wahloo and Maj Sjowall. Photography: David Walsh. 112 minutes.
Cast: Walter Matthau, Bruce Dern, Lou Gossett, Albert

Paulsen, Anthony Zerbe, Val Avery, Cathy Lee Crosby, Mario Gallo, Joanna Cassidy, Shirley Ballard, William Hansen, Jonas Wolfe.

Matthau as homicide detective Jake Martin.

The Taking of Pelham One Two Three (1974)

A Palomar/Palladium Production. Director: Joseph Sargent. Producers: Gabriel Katzka and Edgar J. Sherrick. Screenplay: Peter Stone from the novel by John Godey. Photography: Owen Roizman. 104 minutes.

Cast: Walter Matthau, Robert Shaw, Martin Balsam, Hector Elizondo, Tony Roberts, James Broderick, Dick O'Neill, Lee Wallace, Tom Pedi, Kenneth McMillan, Lucy Saroyan.

Matthau as transit authority lieutenant Garber.

Earthquake (1974)

A Universal Production. Director/Producer: Mark Robson. Screenplay: George Fox and Mario Puzo. Photography: Philip Lathrop. 123 minutes.

Cast: Charlton Heston, Ava Gardner, George Kennedy, Lorne Greene, Genevieve Bujold, Richard Roundtree, Marjoe Gortner, Barry Sullivan, Lloyd Nolan, Victoria Principal, Walter Matuschanskayasky.

Matuschanskayasky (Matthau) as the token drunk.

The Front Page (1974)

A Universal Production. Director: Billy Wilder. Producer: Paul Monash. Screenplay: Billy Wilder and I.A.L. Diamond from the play by Ben Hecht and Charles MacArthur. Photography: Jordan S. Cronenwerth. 105 minutes.

Cast: Jack Lemmon, Walter Matthau, Carol Burnett, Susan Sarandon, Vincent Gardenia, David Wayne,

Allen Garfield*, Austin Pendleton, Charles Durning, Herbert Edelman, Cliff Osmond.

Matthau as Walter Burns, scheming newspaper editor.

THE SUNSHINE BOYS (1975)
A Rastar Production. Director: Herbert Ross. Producer: Ray Stark. Screenplay: Neil Simon from his play. Photography: David M. Walsh. 111 minutes.
Cast: Walter Matthau, George Burns, Richard Benjamin, Lee Meredith, Carol Arthur, Rosetta Le Noire, F. Murray Abraham, Howard Hesseman, Jim Crane, Ron Rifkin, Jennifer Lee.

Matthau as veteran vaudevillian Willy Clark.

THE GENTLEMAN TRAMP (1975)
A Time Incorporated Production. Director/Screenplay: Richard Patterson. Producer: Bert Schneider. 80 minutes.

Matthau, Jack Lemmon and Laurence Olivier narrate this feature-length documentary on the life of Charles Chaplin.

THE BAD NEWS BEARS (1976)
A Paramount Production. Director: Michael Ritchie. Producer: Stanley R. Jaffe. Screenplay: Bill Lancaster. Photography: John Alonzo. 102 minutes.
Cast: Walter Matthau, Tatum O'Neal, Vic Morrow, Joyce Van Patten, Ben Piazza, Jackie Earle Haley, Alfred W. Lutter, Brandon Cruz, Shari Summers, Joe Brooks, Maurice Marks, Quinn Smith.

Matthau as down-at-heel coach Morris Buttermaker.

CASEY'S SHADOW (1978)
A Rastar Production. Director: Martin Ritt. Producer:

* later known as Allen Goorwitz

Ray Stark. Screenplay: Carol Sobieski. Photography:
John Alonzo. 116 minutes.
Cast: Walter Matthau, Alexis Smith, Robert Webber,
Murray Hamilton, Andrew Rubin, Stephen Burns,
Susan Myers, Michael Hershewe, Harry Caesar, Joel
Fluellen, Whit Bissell.
   Matthau as Cajun horse-trainer Lloyd Bourdell.

HOUSE CALLS (1978)

A Universal Production. Director: Howard Zieff.
Producers: Alex Winitsky and Arlene Sellers. Screen-
play: Max Schulman, Julius J. Epstein, Alan Mandel and
Charles Shyer. Photography: David M. Walsh. 98
minutes.
Cast: Walter Matthau, Glenda Jackson, Art Carney,
Richard Benjamin, Candice Azzara, Dick O'Neill,
Thayer David, Anthony Holland, Reva Rose, Sandra
Kerns, Brad Dexter, Charlie Matthau.
   Matthau as widower Dr Charley Nichols.

CALIFORNIA SUITE (1978)

A Rastar Production. Director: Herbert Ross. Producer:
Ray Stark. Screenplay: Neil Simon from his play.
Photography: David M. Walsh. 103 minutes.
Cast: Alan Alda, Michael Caine, Bill Cosby, Jane Fonda,
Walter Matthau, Elaine May, Richard Pryor, Maggie
Smith, James Coburn, Gloria Gifford, Sheila Frazier,
Herbert Edelman, David Matthau.
   Matthau as hapless husband Marvin Michaels.

LITTLE MISS MARKER (1980)

A Universal Production. Director/Screenplay: Walter
Bernstein from a story by Damon Runyon. Producer:
Jennings Lang. Photography: Philip Lathrop. 103
minutes.

Cast: Walter Matthau, Julie Andrews, Tony Curtis, Bob Newhart, Lee Grant, Sara Stimson, Brian Dennehy, Kenneth McMillan, Andrew Rubin, Joshua Shelley, Randy Herman.

Matthau as Depression-era bookie Sorrowful Jones.

HOPSCOTCH (1980)

A Landau Production. Director: Ronald Neame. Producers: Edie and Ely Landau. Screenplay: Brian Garfield and Bryan Forbes from the book by Garfield. Photography: Arthur Ibbetson. 104 minutes.

Cast: Walter Matthau, Glenda Jackson, Sam Waterson, Ned Beatty, Herbert Lom, David Matthau, George Baker, Ivor Roberts, Lucy Saroyan, Severn Darden, George Pravda.

Matthau as super-spy Miles Kendig.

PORTRAIT OF A 60% PERFECT MAN (1980)

An Action Film Production. Director: Annie Tresgot. Producer: Action Film. 58 minutes.

Matthau and Jack Lemmon appear in conversation with French critic Michel Ciment in this feature-length portrait/interview with Billy Wilder.

THE FIRST MONDAY IN OCTOBER (1981)

A Paramount Production. Director: Ronald Neame. Producers: Paul Heller and Martha Scott. Screenplay: Jerome Lawrence and Robert E. Lee from their play. Photography: Fred J. Koenekamp. 95 minutes.

Cast: Walter Matthau, Jill Clayburgh, Barnard Hughes, Jan Sterling, James Stephens, Joshua Bryant, Wiley Parker, F. J. O'Neil, Charles Lampkin, Lew Palter, Richard McMurray.

Matthau as Supreme Court Justice Dan Snow.

BUDDY, BUDDY (1981)
A MGM/United Artists Production. Director: Billy
Wilder. Producer: Jay Weston. Screenplay: Billy Wilder
and I.A.L. Diamond from the play and story by Francis
Veber. Photography: Harry Stradling Jnr. 96 minutes.
Cast: Jack Lemmon, Walter Matthau, Paula Prentiss,
Klaus Kinski, Dana Elcar, Miles Chapin, Michael Ensign,
Joan Shawlee, Fil Formicola, C.J. Hunt, Bette Raya.
    Matthau as hit-man Trabucco.

I OUGHT TO BE IN PICTURES (1982)
A Twentieth Century-Fox Production. Director: Herbert
Ross. Producers: Herbert Ross and Neil Simon.
Screenplay: Neil Simon from his play. Photography:
David M. Walsh. 108 minutes.
Cast: Walter Matthau, Ann Margret, Dinah Manoff,
Lance Guest, Lewis Smith, Martin Ferrero, Eugene
Butler, Samantha Harper, David Faustino, Shelby Belik,
Bill Cross.
    Matthau as Hollywood screenwriter Herbert Tucker.

THE SURVIVORS (1983)
A Rastar-William Sackheim Production. Director:
Michael Ritchie. Producer: William Sackheim.
Screenplay: Michael Leeson. Photography: Billy
Williams.
Cast: Walter Matthau, Robin Williams, Jerry Reed,
James Wainwright, Kristen Vigard, Annie McEnroe,
Anne Pitoniak, Bernard Barrow, Marian Hailey, Joseph
Carberry.
    Matthau as gas-station owner Sonny Paluso.

(Matthau's brief appearance in *King: A Filmed Record*
(1970), a documentary on the life of Martin Luther King,
was edited from the final release print.)

Stage Work
(Selected appearances)

1946/47
THREE MEN ON A HORSE
TEN NIGHTS IN A BAR ROOM

1947/48
THE LITTLE FOXES

1948
ANNE OF A THOUSAND DAYS

1949
THE LIAR

1950
SEASON IN THE SUN

1951
TWILIGHT WALK
ONE BRIGHT DAY
FANCY MEETING YOU AGAIN

1952
IN ANY LANGUAGE
GREY-EYED PEOPLE

1953
LADIES OF THE CORRIDOR

1955
WISTERIA TREES
GUYS AND DOLLS
WILL SUCCESS SPOIL ROCK
    HUNTER?

1956
MAIDEN VOYAGE

1958
ONCE MORE WITH FEELING

1960
ONCE THERE WAS A RUSSIAN

1961/62
A SHOT IN THE DARK

1964/65
THE ODD COUPLE

1974
JUNO AND THE PAYCOCK

Television Appearances

(A Selected Chronology adapted from Actors' Television Credits by James Robert Parish.)

1952

Tour of Duty	(TV Playhouse)
Straight Forward Narrow	(Armstrong Circle Theatre)
The Basket Weaver	(Philco Playhouse)
Should Doctors Ever Marry?	(Schlitz Playhouse)
A Buck is a Buck	(Danger)
Death of Kid Slawson	(Kraft Theatre)
Three Sundays	(Goodyear Playhouse)

1953

Hand Me Down	(Danger)
F.O.B. Vienna	(Suspense)
Nightmare Number Three	(Plymouth Playhouse)
Nothing to Sneeze At	(Goodyear Playhouse)
The New Process	(Goodyear Playhouse)
Wonder In Your Eyes	(TV Sound Stage)
Othello	(Philco Playhouse)
Dry Run	(Studio One)
The Glorification of Al Toolum	(Philco Playhouse)

1954

Love Date	(US Steel Hour)
Atomic Attack	(TV Hour)
Adapt or Die	(Philco Playhouse)

The Human Touch	(Center Stage)
Flight Report	(Goodyear Playhouse)
Dr Ed	(Robert Montgomery Presents)

1955

Walk Into the Night	(Philco Playhouse)
A Westerner's Race Prejudice	(Robert Montgomery Presents)
Bobby Trap	(Justice)
The Lost Weekend	(Robert Montgomery)

1956

| The Big Vote | (Alcoa Hour) |

1957

A Will to Live	(Goodyear Playhouse)
The Legacy	(Goodyear Playhouse)
The Trouble with Women	(Alcoa Hour)
To Walk the Night	(Climax)

1958

| Code of the Corner | (Kraft Theatre) |
| The Crooked Road | (Alfred Hitchcock Presents) |

1959

| Tallahassee 7000 (series) | (Alfred Hitchcock Presents) |
| Dry Run | |

1960

Juno and the Paycock	(Play of the Week)
The Rope Dancers	(Play of the Week)
Very Moral Theft	(Alfred Hitchcock Presents)
My Heart's in the Highlands	(Play of the Week)
Born a Giant	(Our American Heritage)
The Man Who Bit the Diamond in Half	(Naked City)

1961

| Eleven, the Hard Way | (Route 66) |

| The Million Dollar Dump | (Target: Corrupters) |
| Cop for a Day | (Alfred Hitchcock Theatre) |

1962
Footnote to Fame	(Westinghouse Presents)
Acres and Pains	(G.E. Theatre)
Big Deal in Laredo	(Dupont Show of the Month)
Don't Knock it Till You've Tried It	(Naked City)

1963
| A Tumble from a White Horse | (Eleventh Hour) |
| The Takers | (Dupont Show of the Month) |

1964
White Snow, Red Ice	(Bob Hope Chrysler Theatre)
Jeremy Rabbitt, the Secret Avenger	(Dupont Show of the Month)
The Personal Touch	(The Rogues)
Man is Rock	(Dr Kildare)

1965
| Andrew Johnson | (Profiles in Courage) |

1967
| Jack Benny's Bag | (Guest appearance) |

1972
| Awake and Sing | (Hollywood Television Theatre) |

1978
Hollywood Television Theatre
Insight
| The Stingiest Man in Town | (Voice only) |
| Funny Business | (Narrator) |

1982
| Hollywood: The Gift of Laughter | (Narrator) |

Bibliography

Books

Blatake, Joe   *The Films of Jack Lemmon* (USA: Citadel Press 1977)

Bowles, Stephen E.   *Sidney Lumet: A Guide to References and Resources* (USA: G.K. Hall & Co. 1979)

Burns, George   *Living It Up* (UK: W.H. Allen 1977)

Harrison, Rex   *Rex: An Autobiography* (UK: Macmillan 1974)

Hirschhorn, Clive   *The Films of James Mason* (UK: LSP 1975)

Mason, James   *Before I Forget* (UK: Hamish Hamilton 1981)

Steinberg, Cobbett   *Reel Facts* (USA: Vintage Books 1978)

Teichman, Howard   *Fonda – My Life* (UK: W.H. Allen 1982)

Thomas, Tony   *The Films of Kirk Douglas* (USA: Citadel Press 1972)

    The Films of Gene Kelly (USA: Citadel Press 1974)

Widener, Don   *Lemmon: A Biography* (UK: W.H. Allen 1977)

Willett, John   *The Theatre of Erwin Piscator* (UK: Eyre Methuen 1976)

Zolotow, Maurice   *Billy Wilder in Hollywood* (UK: W.H. Allen 1977)

Articles

Crawley, Tony   'The Bison of the Hollywood Veldt' (*Films Illustrated*, February 1980)

D'Arcy, Susan   'Making *The Front Page* – The Wilder Way' (*Films Illustrated*, February 1975)

Goodman, Joan & Bygrave, Mike   Mr Matthau's Business' (*Observer Magazine*, 4/2/79)

Hall, William 'Walter Matthau – at the top but a born loser'
  (*Evening News*, 30/7/68)

Hirschhorn, Clive 'How shy Mr Matthau fools everybody'
  (*Sunday Express*, 28/9/80)

McAsh, Iain F. '*Hopscotch* – Matthau and Jackson jump at a
  reunion' (*Films Illustrated*, January 1980)

Mann, Roderick 'Matthau's melancholy' (*Sunday Express*,
  4/9/81)

Owen, Michael 'Not a Pretty Face, Thank God' (*The Evening
  Standard*, 9/1/76)

Sandilands, John 'Hello, Walter' (*Daily Mirror*, 11/12/69)

Schickel, Richard 'Beleagured Sanity Toughs It Out' (*Time*,
  4/7/83)

Zec, Donald 'You Can Bet On That' (*Daily Mirror*, 28/5/76)

Index

205

207